# Harrowing of the Heart

## The Poetry of Bloody Sunday

A collection of poetry, song and drama
inspired by events in Derry on 30 January 1972

*For Trisha,
A little moments of Derry...
With love from,
[signature] Jenny + Nina.
xo*

Edited by
Julieann Campbell and Tom Herron

**GUILDHALL PRESS**

First published in January 2008

Guildhall Press
Ráth Mór Business Park
Bligh's Lane
Derry BT48 0LZ
T: (028) 7136 4413 F: (028) 7137 2949
info@ghpress.com  www.ghpress.com

A CIP catalogue record for this book is available from the
British Library.

The authors assert their moral rights in this work in accordance with
the Copyright, Designs and Patents Act 1998.

Cover photograph © Robert White

Typeset by Kevin Hippsley and Joe McAllister
General editor: Paul Hippsley
Cover design and illustration by David Campbell
Copyright © Authors / Guildhall Press
ISBN: 978 1 906271 08 4

Lyrics from Sunday Bloody Sunday by John Lennon and Yoko Ono
kindly reproduced with the permission of Lenono Music.

Lyrics from Minds Locked Shut by Christy Moore kindly reproduced
with the permission of Columbia UK.

All rights reserved. No part of this publication may be reproduced or transmitted in any
form or by any means, electronic or mechanical, including photocopy, recording, or any
information storage or retrieval system, without permission in writing from the publisher.
The book is sold subject to the condition that it shall not, by way of trade or otherwise,
be lent, resold or otherwise circulated without the publisher's prior consent in any form of
binding or cover other than that in which it is published and without a similar condition
this condition being imposed on the subsequent purchaser.

*Dedicated to the fallen and wounded
of Bloody Sunday*

# The Dead and Wounded of Bloody Sunday, 30 January 1972

**Dead:**

Patrick Doherty (31)
Gerald Donaghey (17)
Jackie Duddy (17)
Hugh Gilmour (17)
Michael Kelly (17)
Michael McDaid (20)
Kevin McElhinney (17)
Bernard McGuigan (41)
Gerard McKinney (35)
William McKinney (27)
William Nash (19)
James Wray (22)
John Young (17)
John Johnston (59, died 16 June 1972)

**Wounded:**

Michael Bradley
Michael Bridge
Alana Burke
Patrick Campbell
Margaret Deery
Damien Donaghy
Joseph Friel
Danny Gillespie
Joseph Mahon
Patrick McDaid
Daniel McGowan
Alex Nash
Patrick O'Donnell
Michael Quinn

## Acknowledgements

This collection would not have been possible without the support of so many people, primarily the contributors who entrusted us with their work and allowed us to commit their words to paper. We also would like to extend our thanks to the following:

Seamus Heaney for allowing us to use his resonant phrase for the title of this book.

Bishop Edward Daly for his insightful foreword.

Paul Hippsley, Declan Carlin and everyone at Guildhall Press for their empathy towards the spirit of the idea and their commitment to its realisation.

Colleagues at the *Derry Journal* for their continuous support and for allowing access to the paper's archives.

John Kelly and Adrian Kerr at the Museum of Free Derry for invaluable help, advice and access to the museum archives. The relatives of Bloody Sunday, many of whom gave freely of their time to advise and assist us on this project. Eamonn McCann and the Bloody Sunday Trust.

Juliet, Seamus and Fergal for their constant support, interest, and much-needed distraction. Susie and the Campbell boys for all their support and encouragement. Kay Duddy, Mama Cass, Paula, Aisling and Brenda for their listening ear. Christopher, for always being there.

Robert White for his stunning cover photograph and David Campbell for his wonderful illustration and cover design.

Donncha MacNiallais at An Gaelaras for the translation of *Obráid Domhnach Na Fola/Operation Bloody Sunday*.

Ross Moore of the Northern Ireland Political Collection at Belfast's Linen Hall Library.

The publishers and record companies for permission to reproduce several of these works: Peppercanister Press, Columbia UK, Faber & Faber, Lenono Music, Anvil Press and Carcanet Press.

# Foreword

The title of this anthology, *Harrowing of the Heart*, is taken from Seamus Heaney's speech when he accepted the Nobel Prize in Literature in Stockholm in 1995. It is a perceptive and accurate metaphor for the type of suffering and anguish that people experienced during our years of conflict here.

This anthology of poetry and song focuses on the events of one cold and cruel January afternoon in Derry, events about which much has been written. Those events have been re-enacted, recreated and recalled on many occasions in prose, poetry, song, theatre and film.

Poets are the princes of literature. William Wordsworth once wrote: 'Poetry is the spontaneous overflow of powerful feelings; it takes its origin from emotion recollected in tranquillity.'

In this anthology, various writers express their anger and dismay and distress at the shameful events of that day. They give expression to that 'spontaneous overflow of powerful feelings' that Wordsworth wrote about.

The harrow is a crude agricultural tool that tears up ground and leaves it broken and tattered. However, in so doing, the harrow prepares ground for seed and a new crop and new life.

I would like to think that the acknowledgment of the awful reality and pain of the harrowing days and years that all sides have experienced will prepare the ground to nurture and encourage the new life and hope that we are now beginning to experience in the North.

That must be our anticipation today as we face into a new millennium.

**Bishop Edward Daly**
**November 2007**

## INTRODUCTION

When we first embarked upon this project, we presumed we would gather a modest collection of local poetry inspired by the events of 30 January 1972. Instead, our research has uncovered a rich and deeply personal body of work capturing the horror and anguish of Bloody Sunday and its devastating legacy on an entire city.

Many of the writers included in this book witnessed Derry's greatest atrocity first hand, others are relatives of those killed, and some were not yet born when British Paratroopers entered the Bogside that Sunday afternoon, killing thirteen and wounding a further fifteen. Regardless of the intensely private experiences of each contributor, however, they share one common aspect: an indelible impression left by Bloody Sunday and a need to express this lingering sense of disbelief through the written word.

No single event, no comparable atrocity of the Northern Irish conflict, has provoked the number and diversity of artistic responses as the pieces collected within the covers of this book attest. Why should this be? Whilst Bloody Sunday was a pivotal moment in the Northern Ireland Troubles, it was part of a constellation of violence that caused immense pain and long-term suffering to people of all parties, factions and sides of the conflict: as well, of course, to those entirely non-aligned victims. So, it is worthwhile asking the question why – of all the harrowings of the heart that scarred the North of Ireland and beyond such as the horrors of McGurk's Bar, Bloody Friday, the Dublin/Monaghan bombings, Birmingham, Darkley, Enniskillen, Greysteel, Omagh and so many others – has Bloody Sunday attracted the number and the diversity of poetic, dramatic, and lyrical responses?

In his book *The Bloody Sunday Inquiry: the Families Speak Out*, activist Eamonn McCann notes:

> A number of things made Derry different. This was a very British atrocity, and the biggest single killing by state forces in the course of the Troubles. The resultant affront was compounded by the fact that the British state at the highest level, in the person of the Lord Chief Justice, had then proclaimed that the killings were neither wrong nor illegal. In every other atrocity with which Bloody Sunday has regularly been compared or likened, the victims are acknowledged, more or less universally, as having been wrongly done to death and the perpetrators damned as wrongdoers. But the Bloody Sunday families were told, in effect, that while they might personally, reasonably, lament the loss of a loved one, they had no wider ground for grievance or legitimate expectation of the killers being punished. The state stood by its own. All the dead were thus diminished.

Frustrated at the lack of recognition or admission of guilt from the British Government, the people of Derry themselves found alternative means of remembering their collective loss and highlighting their demands for truth and justice through annual commemoration events.

The new Bloody Sunday Inquiry, chaired by Lord Saville, is the first serious attempt by the British Government to engage in the issues that have long since haunted them. The actions of 1 Para proved to be the catalyst for myriad consequences, as embittered youths flocked to join the IRA, intent on a revolution. Bloody Sunday marked the turning point in Northern Ireland's conflict and perpetuated the utter disenchantment felt by many.

With a wealth of prose, newspaper editorial, eyewitness and personal accounts still out there, this collection is by no means a definitive account of Bloody Sunday. Nor could we hope to have found every poetic response. However, this book – that we envisage as a sort of archive – does provide an invaluable insight into how a selection of Irish poets, dramatists, and musicians perceived the events that transpired on the streets of Derry on a cold, crisp day in January.

But how did we come across these mostly unseen works of local literature? With several notable works such as Seamus Heaney's *Casualty*, Thomas Kinsella's *Butcher's Dozen* and Lennon and Ono's song *Sunday Bloody Sunday* already in the public domain, we were tasked to uncover more poetic responses from the people of Derry themselves. Several well-placed articles in the *Derry Journal* seeking local pieces about Bloody Sunday helped our search considerably, with dozens of poems and songs streaming in from throughout the North West and beyond.

Overwhelmed by the response and by the goodwill of those who responded, we realised this was not just any collection of poetry – this was a vivid account of local history captured by the people themselves. Indeed, every writer we approached in the hope of permission was equally generous and more than willing to have their work included in our collection.

No doubt there are other poetic jewels about Bloody Sunday still waiting to be discovered; no doubt there will be many more to write before this chapter is closed by Lord Saville. But until then we endeavour to pay tribute to, and commemorate, Derry's dead and injured through the eyes of poets, playwrights, and songwriters. Painstakingly sought out more than three decades after the events of Bloody Sunday, this hugely significant collection speaks from the heart and the soul of each and every author.

Committed to paper, these poems bear witness to the unity and strength shown by a community in mourning. In their own unique way, they reflect the means by which an entire city struggled to cope with the unimaginable events thrust upon them.

We hope that this collection will be afforded its own place among the colossal archive of the Troubles, enlightening and educating future generations about a past now hopefully behind us.

**Julieann Campbell and Tom Herron**

## Contents

| | | |
|---|---|---|
| Derry's Thirteen | KATHLEEN PATTON | 17 |
| The Road to Derry | SEAMUS HEANEY | 19 |
| Untitled | JAMES WRAY | 20 |
| McGuigan | MARY J DEVLIN | 21 |
| Bloody Sunday, 30 January 1972 | EUGENE DUFFY | 22 |
| Bloody Sunday | MICHAEL MCLAUGHLIN | 23 |
| Butcher's Dozen: A Lesson for the Octave of Widgery | THOMAS KINSELLA | 24 |
| After Derry, 30 January 1972 | SEAMUS DEANE | 31 |
| Sunday Bloody Sunday | JOHN LENNON & YOKO ONO | 33 |
| Bloody Sunday | JOE MULHERON | 35 |
| Rossville Street Sunday | DA WILLIE FOLK | 36 |
| Bloody Sunday | PEGGY GOUGH | 38 |
| Untitled | ANONYMOUS | 39 |
| Anniversary | JOE MCGRORY | 40 |
| The Freedom of the City (extract) | BRIAN FRIEL | 41 |
| The Year of the Sloes, For Ishi | PAUL MULDOON | 43 |
| Derry | MARY J DEVLIN | 47 |
| Casualty | SEAMUS HEANEY | 48 |
| Bloody Sunday | HUGH GALLAGHER | 52 |

| | | |
|---|---|---|
| Bloody Sunday | Hugh Gallagher | 54 |
| Counting the Dead on the Radio | Thomas McCarthy | 55 |
| Sunday Stones | L Morris | 57 |
| Carthaginians (extract) | Frank McGuinness | 59 |
| Marchers | Eoghan MacCormaic | 64 |
| Obráid Domhnach Na Fola / Operation Bloody Sunday | Dan Baron Cohen/ Derry Frontline | 65&67 |
| Let the Stones Speak | Emmylou Large | 69 |
| Sunday, Bloody Sunday | Tommy Sands | 71 |
| Bloody Sunday Revisited | Anonymous | 72 |
| Remembering Bloody Sunday | Paul Laughlin | 74 |
| Looking Back to the Future | Jackie Duddy | 75 |
| William Nash | Amanda C Rowe | 77 |
| Minds Locked Shut | Christy Moore | 78 |
| I Wasn't Even Born | Sharon Meenan & Killian Mullan | 80 |
| Running Uphill | Declan McLaughlin | 81 |
| Injustice | John F McCartney | 83 |
| The Grief of Derry | Jackie Duddy | 84 |
| Tribute to Lord Fenner-Brockway | John Dunne | 85 |
| That Fateful Day | Martin Wray | 87 |
| A Disarming Suggestion | Perry McDaid | 89 |
| They Were Better Than Most | Paddy McCourt | 90 |

| | | |
|---|---|---|
| Uncle Jackie | PAUL CAMPBELL | 91 |
| No Longer Cry | ROBERT MCDAID & PATRICK O'DOHERTY | 92 |
| Pablo's Part | JULIEANN CAMPBELL | 93 |
| The Story of Bloody Sunday in Verse (extract) | JP MCMENAMIN | 94 |
| Muted Martyrs | PERRY MCDAID | 97 |
| One Sunday | GERRY DORRITY | 98 |
| 1 Para | SCOTT MX TURNER | 100 |
| William Street, Derry, January 2002 (After Yeats et al) | BERNI KERR | 103 |
| My Role Was That of an Observer (General Robert Ford) | MARY O'MALLEY | 104 |
| Monday, 31 January 1972 | TONY RAMSAY | 105 |
| Scenes From an Inquiry (extract) | DAVE DUGGAN | 108 |
| Herm | PAUL MULDOON | 110 |
| Maire – A Woman of Derry (extract) | BRIAN FOSTER | 111 |
| The Day Innocents Died | MICHAEL WILLIAM BENSON | 114 |
| A Long Auld Walk (extract) | LAURENCE MCCLENAGHAN | 115 |
| The Thief in the Night | PAUL CAMPBELL | 120 |
| Futility Reigns | AARON PHELAN | 122 |
| Reluctant Role Model | JULIEANN CAMPBELL | 123 |
| Bloody Sunday | CHARLIE MCLAUGHLIN | 124 |
| Heroes With Their Hands in the Air (extract) | FINTAN BRADY & EAMONN MCCANN | 125 |
| I Am Told | NIALL KELLY | 129 |
| The Writers | | 131 |

# Derry's Thirteen

*Kathleen Patton (1972)*

In St Colmcille's dear city,
'Neath a dark and dreary sky,
Irishmen were brutally murdered.
By British guns these young men died.

They had marched against Internment
In a quiet and peaceful way.
This didn't suit the Paratroopers –
They were out to kill that day.

Then their mad bloodthirsty general
Called his men to shoot and kill.
He blamed it on the snipers,
Saying they fired first from o'er the hill.

When that bloody day was over
Thirteen Derry men lay dead.
Lots more of them lay injured,
Colmcille's loved streets ran red.

There was sixteen-year-old Kelly,
Two McKinneys and young Nash,
Joe McDaid, Joe Wray and Gilmour,
Murdered in that bloody dash.

There was Doherty and McGuigan,
McElhinney and Donaghey, too,
John Young and Jackie Duddy.
British butchery – nothing new.

Add these men to Ireland's martyrs.
A jewel of shame to England's crown.
For cunning, lies and propaganda
British troops are world renowned.

God rest those sons of Derry.
Pray their deaths shall be the last.
That soon we'll hear all Irish voices
Thanking God there's peace at last.

# The Road to Derry

*Seamus Heaney (1972)*

On a Wednesday morning early I took the road to Derry
Along Glenshane and Foreglen and the cold woods of Hillhead;
A wet wind in the hedges and a dark cloud on the mountain
And flags like black frost mourning that thirteen men were dead.

The Roe wept at Dungiven and the Foyle cried out to heaven,
Burntollet's old wound opened and again the Bogside bled;
By Shipquay Gate I shivered and by Lone Moor I enquired
Where I might find the coffins where the thirteen men lay dead.

My heart besieged by anger, my mind a gap of danger,
I walked among their old haunts, the home ground where they bled;
And in the dirt lay justice like an acorn in the winter
Till its oak would sprout in Derry where the thirteen men lay dead.

# Untitled

*James Wray (1972)*

I'm a First Battalion Paratrooper
And for me the future is black
There in the Bogside on Sunday
I shot a young man in the back.

He was unarmed and running for shelter
As we went in to attack
I pressed my finger on the trigger
And shot a young man in the back.

The Cabinet in England gave the order
And for that they should get the sack
Like Judas I got a few shillings
So I shot a young man in the back.

I was unknown to those who were present
Who looked round when they heard the crack
But this is no ease to my conscience
For I shot a young man in the back.

Through life I must keep my dark secret
And that's why my future is black
Can't confide to my mother or sweetheart
That I shot a young man in the back.

And when it's my time to be dying
I know that my thoughts will go back
To the Bogside that Bloody Sunday
When I shot a young man in the back.

## McGuigan *(to the air of The Butcher Boy)*
*Mary J Devlin (1972)*

It was the march for Civil Rights,
Twenty thousand marched from Creggan Heights.
They assembled in the old Bogside
And that is where McGuigan died.

In the bright sunshine the crowd did stand.
All for the cause of Fatherland.
No warning given, shots rang out
They hit their targets, there was no doubt.

A bullet pierced McGuigan's head.
A noble man he fell there dead.
A friend ran forward to his aid
Of British soldiers not afraid.

McGuigan lay there like a cross
Another martyr for the cause,
The pavement was his dying bed,
With no soft pillow for his head.

One of the brave, killed in the fray
Killed in Derry on Bloody Sunday.
On Bloody Sunday of seventy-two,
He died for me, he died for you.

# Bloody Sunday, 30 January 1972

*Eugene Duffy (1972)*

'Twas the thirtieth of January in Derry, thousands marched for Civil Rights
From the top shops in Creggan, high up there in the heights.
The procession it was joyous, friendly but sincere.
No doubt the army presence was definitely here.
Our songs for justice were loud, clear and sweet
As we marched along the Moor to the corner of Rossville Street!
Then suddenly, shots rang out, the sound was loud and clear.
Boys and girls, husbands and wives ran, running for their lives.
A young man lay still, his father by his side,
As the British advanced with licences to kill.
One, two three, four more lay dead. 'It's terrible,' some old lady said.
'Kill all the Fenian bastards,' a Paratrooper yelled,
'We won't take long until we have this riot quelled.'
Another boy lay dead at the corner of the street,
And the Paras dragged him away like a dog by the feet!
And when the shooting ended at Mass time we were told
Fourteen men and boys lay motionless and cold.
Dear God, please don't let them die for nothing,
Bloody Sunday can never be forgotten.

# Bloody Sunday

*Michael McLaughlin (1972)*

I remember fifty years ago, a very sorry day,
Bloody Sunday in Croke Park and it seemed so far away.
No news was flashed across our screens as news is flashed today,
But when the word came out the next day the world stood in dismay
At the bloody deeds in Dublin committed by the Crown.
They went in like crazy savages and shot the people down.
An old man stood beside me, shocked by these awful deeds,
He got us all to stand around and pray upon our beads.
We prayed for all who died that day and all who died before.
We asked the Lord to give them rest and peace for evermore.

Now we have another Bloody Sunday in our own beloved town,
When once again like savages they shot the people down.
I stood beside those thirteen graves designed to hold the dead,
And like that old man long ago, I bowed my weary head.
I prayed for all who died that day and all who died before,
I prayed that God would give them rest and peace for evermore.

I also said another prayer as said today by few,
I said, 'O, Lord, forgive them, for they know not what they do.'

# Butcher's Dozen: A Lesson for the Octave of Widgery

*Thomas Kinsella (1972)*

I went with Anger at my heel
Through Bogside of the bitter zeal
– Jesus pity! – on a day
Of cold and drizzle and decay.
A month had passed. Yet there remained
A murder smell that stung and stained.
On flats and alleys – over all –
It hung; on battered roof and wall,
On wreck and rubbish scattered thick,
On sullen steps and pitted brick.
And when I came where thirteen died
It shrivelled up my heart. I sighed
And looked about that brutal place
Of rage and terror and disgrace.
Then my moistened lips grew dry.
I had heard an answering sigh!
There in a ghostly pool of blood
A crumpled phantom hugged the mud:
'Once there lived a hooligan.
A pig came up, and away he ran.
Here lies one in blood and bones,
Who lost his life for throwing stones.'

More voices rose. I turned and saw
Three corpses forming, red and raw,
From dirt and stone. Each upturned face
Stared unseeing from its place:
'Behind this barrier, blighters three,
We scrambled back and made to flee.

The guns cried Stop, and here lie we.'
Then from left and right they came,
More mangled corpses, bleeding, lame,
Holding their wounds. They chose their ground,
Ghost by ghost, without a sound,
And one stepped forward, soiled and white:
'A bomber I. I travelled light
– Four pounds of nails and gelignite
About my person, hid so well
They seemed to vanish where I fell.
When the bullet stopped my breath
A doctor sought the cause of death.
He upped my shirt, undid my fly,
Twice he moved my limbs awry,
And noticed nothing. By and by
A soldier, with his sharper eye,
Beheld the four elusive rockets
Stuffed in my coat and trouser pockets.
Yes, they must be strict with us,
Even in death so treacherous!'
He faded, and another said:
'We three met close when we were dead.
Into an armoured car they piled us
Where our mingled blood defiled us,
Certain, if not dead before,
To suffocate upon the floor.

Careful bullets in the back
Stopped our terrorist attack,
And so three dangerous lives are done
– Judged, condemned and shamed in one.'
That spectre faded in his turn.
A harsher stirred, and spoke in scorn:
'The shame is theirs, in word and deed,

Who prate of justice, practise greed,
And act in ignorant fury – then,
Officers and gentlemen,
Send to their Courts for the Most High
To tell us did we really die!
Does it need recourse to law
To tell ten thousand what they saw?
Law that lets them, caught red-handed,
Halt the game and leave it stranded,
Summon up a sworn inquiry
And dump their conscience in the diary.
During which hiatus, should
Their legal basis vanish, good,
The thing is rapidly arranged:
Where's the law that can't be changed?
The news is out. The troops were kind.
Impartial justice has to find
We'd be alive and well today
If we had let them have their way.
Yet England, even as you lie,
You give the facts that you deny.
Spread the lie with all your power
– All that's left; it's turning sour.
Friend and stranger, bride and brother,
Son and sister, father, mother,
All not blinded by your smoke,
Photographers who caught your stroke,
The priests that blessed our bodies, spoke
And wagged our blood in the world's face.
The truth will out, to your disgrace.'
He flushed and faded. Pale and grim,
A joking spectre followed him:
'Take a bunch of stunted shoots,
A tangle of transplanted roots,
Ropes and rifles, feathered nests,

Some dried colonial interests,
A hard unnatural union grown
In a bed of blood and bone,
Tongue of serpent, gut of hog
Spiced with spleen of underdog.
Stir in, with oaths of loyalty,
Sectarian supremacy,
And heat, to make a proper botch,
In a bouillon of bitter Scotch.
Last, the choice ingredient: you.
Now, to crown your Irish stew,
Boil it over, make a mess.
A most imperial success!'
He capered weakly, racked with pain,
His dead hair plastered in the rain;
The group was silent once again.
It seemed the moment to explain
That sympathetic politicians
Say our violent traditions,
Backward looks and bitterness
Keep us in this dire distress.
We must forget, and look ahead,

Nurse the living, not the dead.
My words died out. A phantom said:
'Here lies one who breathed his last
Firmly reminded of the past.
A trooper did it, on one knee,
In tones of brute authority.'
That harsher spirit, who before
Had flushed with anger, spoke once more:
'Simple lessons cut most deep.
This lesson in our hearts we keep:
Persuasion, protest, arguments,
The milder forms of violence,

Earn nothing but polite neglect.
England, the way to your respect
Is via murderous force, it seems;
You push us to your own extremes.
You condescend to hear us speak
Only when we slap your cheek.
And yet we lack the last technique:
We rap for order with a gun,
The issues simplify to one
– Then your Democracy insists
You mustn't talk with terrorists!
White and yellow, black and blue,
Have learnt their history from you:
Divide and ruin, muddle through,
Not principled, but politic.
– In strength, perfidious; weak, a trick
To make good men a trifle sick.
We speak in wounds. Behold this mess.
My curse upon your politesse.'

Another ghost stood forth, and wet
Dead lips that had not spoken yet:
'My curse on the cunning and the bland,
On gentlemen who loot a land
They do not care to understand;
Who keep the natives on their paws
With ready lash and rotten laws;
Then if the beasts erupt in rage
Give them a slightly larger cage
And, in scorn and fear combined,
Turn them against their own kind.
The game runs out of room at last,
A people rises from its past,
The going gets unduly tough
And you have (surely . . . ?) had enough.

The time has come to yield your place
With condescending show of grace
– An Empire-builder handing on.
We reap the ruin when you've gone,
All your errors heaped behind you:
Promises that do not bind you,
Hopes in conflict, cramped commissions,
Faiths exploited, and traditions.'
Bloody sputum filled his throat.
He stopped and coughed to clear it out,
And finished, with his eyes a-glow:
'You came, you saw, you conquered . . . So.
You gorged – and it was time to go.
Good riddance. We'd forget – released –
But for the rubbish of your feast,
The slops and scraps that fell to earth
And sprang to arms in dragon birth.

Sashed and bowler-hatted, glum
Apprentices of fife and drum,
High and dry, abandoned guards
Of dismal streets and empty yards,
Drilled at the codeword 'True Religion'
To strut and mutter like a pigeon
'Not An Inch – Up The Queen';
Who use their walls like a latrine
For scribbled magic – at their call,
Straight from the nearest music-hall,
Pope and Devil intertwine,
Two cardboard kings appear, and join
In one more battle by the Boyne!
Who could love them? God above . . .'
'Yet pity is akin to love,'
The thirteenth corpse beside him said,
Smiling in its bloody head,

'And though there's reason for alarm
In dourness and a lack of charm
Their cursed plight calls out for patience.
They, even they, with other nations
Have a place, if we can find it.
Love our changeling! Guard and mind it.
Doomed from birth, a cursed heir,
Theirs is the hardest lot to bear,
Yet not impossible, I swear,
If England would but clear the air
And brood at home on her disgrace
– Everything to its own place.
Face their walls of dole and fear
And be of reasonable cheer.

Good men every day inherit
Father's foulness with the spirit,
Purge the filth and do not stir it.
Let them out! At least let in
A breath or two of oxygen,
So they may settle down for good
And mix themselves in the common blood.
We are what we are, and that
Is mongrel pure. What nation's not
Where any stranger hung his hat
And seized a lover where she sat?'
He ceased and faded. Zephyr blew
And all the others faded, too.
I stood like a ghost. My fingers strayed
Along the fatal barricade.
The gentle rainfall drifting down
Over Colmcille's town
Could not refresh, only distil
In silent grief from hill to hill.

# After Derry, 30 January 1972

*Seamus Deane (1972)*

Lightnings slaughtered
The distance. In the harmless houses
Faces narrowed. The membrane
Of power darkened
Above the valley,
And in a flood of khaki
Burst. Indigoed
As rain they came
As the thunder radioed
For a further
Haemorrhage of flame.

The roads died, the clocks
Went out. The peace
Had been a delicately flawed
Honeymoon signalling
The fearful marriage
To come. Death had been
A form of doubt.
Now it was moving
Like a missionary
Through the collapsed cities
Converting all it came among.

And when the storm passed
We came out of the back rooms
Wishing we could say
Ruin itself would last.
But the dead would not
Listen. Nor could we speak

Of love. Brothers had been
Pitiless. What could ignite
This sodden night?
Let us bury the corpses.
Fast. Death is our future.

And now is our past.
There are new children
In the gaunt houses.
Their eyes are fused.
Youth has gone out
Like a light. Only the insects
Grovel for life, their strange heads
Twitching. No one kills them
Anymore. This is the honeymoon
Of the cockroach, the small
Spiderless eternity of the fly.

# Sunday Bloody Sunday

*John Lennon and Yoko Ono (1972)*

Well, it was Sunday Bloody Sunday
When they shot the people there
The cries of thirteen martyrs
Filled the Free Derry air.
Is there any one amongst you
Dare to blame it on the kids?
Not a soldier boy was bleeding
When they nailed the coffin lids!

Sunday Bloody Sunday
Bloody Sunday's the day!

You claim to be the majority
Well you know that it's a lie.
You're really a minority
On this sweet emerald isle.
When Stormont bans our marches
They've got a lot to learn.
Internment is no answer
It's those mothers' turn to burn!

Sunday Bloody Sunday
Bloody Sunday's the day!

You Anglo-pigs and Scotties
Sent to colonise the North,
You wave your bloody Union Jack
And you know what it's worth!
How dare you hold to ransom
A people proud and free,
Keep Ireland for the Irish
Put the English back to sea!

Sunday Bloody Sunday
Bloody Sunday's the day!

Well, it's always Bloody Sunday
In the concentration camps,
Keep Falls Road free forever
From the bloody English hands.
Repatriate to Britain
All of you who call it home.
Leave Ireland to the Irish
Not for London or for Rome!

Sunday Bloody Sunday
Bloody Sunday's the day!

# Bloody Sunday

*Joe Mulheron (1972)*

'We demand Civil Rights,' well, the marchers did say,
Ten thousand people assembled that day
For Free Derry Corner, set out with a cheer
The march it was peaceful, there was nothing to fear

But the Paratroop Regiment came down the street
Five hundred men – all over six feet
They carried machine guns and big SLRs
Coming down William Street in their Saracen cars

Well the orders were given in Whitehall we know
Open fire, kill a few, draw them out, have a go
No fire was returned, as the world knows today
Fourteen innocent men with their lives had to pay

At Free Derry Corner the slaughter began
Some people fell and some people ran
The Civil Rights banner was stained bloody red
At the barricades there, they shot three people dead

The wounded lay bleeding, a doctor is called
The firing continues and another two fall
The harvest they reaped with their bullets of lead
Bloody Sunday in Derry and fourteen men dead

The Widgery mockery, it was soon carried out
Just doing their duty, well, there is no doubt
On England's proud history a crime added yet
How can we forgive them? How can we forget?

## Rossville Street Sunday (to the air of *The Patriot Game*)

*Da Willie Folk (1972)*

'And while Ireland holds these graves,
Ireland unfree shall never be at peace.'
**PH Pearse**

*Spoken:*
Jack Duddy, Kevin McElhinney, Barney McGuigan,
Paddy Doherty, Hugh Gilmour, William Nash,
Michael Kelly, Michael McDaid, John Young, Jim Wray,
William McKinney, Gerry McKinney, Gerry Donaghey.

*Sing:*
Come gather round people
and I'll sing you a song,
I'll sing it so softly
it'll do no one wrong,
on Rossville Street Sunday
the blood ran like wine,
of those who were marching
for freedom that day.

That evening was cold
but I saw the sun,
and young Michael Kelly
his number was one,
when the British decided
to shoot everyone,
of those who were marching
for freedom that day.

The priests and the people
they pleaded 'no more,'

but the murders continued
to roll up the score,
by four o'clock there were
ten dead or more,
of those who were marching
for freedom that day.

When they see the slaughter
of the old and the young,
tears flowed from the eyes
of everyone,
on Rossville Street Sunday
there were thirteen gone,
of those who were marching
for freedom that day.

Backs turned to the soldiers
eyes facing the sun,
we witnessed the murders
of fathers and sons,
we'll revenge the death
of our darling young ones,
of those who were marching
for freedom that day.

# Bloody Sunday

*Peggy Gough (1972)*

It started out a peaceful march of twenty thousand strong
And all of them were cheerful as they marched along.

The Civil Rights had ordered a peaceful demonstration
But the Paras planned to massacre, as it neared its destination.

It was just another Sunday, like the one so long ago,
That happened in Croke Park just fifty years ago.

The Paras they were called in to do their dirty work
And from every rooftop a Paratrooper lurked.

They started off with red dye to mark their victims well,
Then opened up with CS gas, rubber bullets and hot lead.

Thousands fled in terror, not knowing where to run
Because it was a Paratrooper who stood behind the gun.

These weren't the men from Arnhem, from whence their glory came,
God help their Commanding Officer, who's not worthy of the name.

And when this bloody deed was done thirteen men lay dead,
Their bodies torn and wounded lay there full of lead.

There are saddened hearts in Derry as we mourn our dead,
They shall never be forgotten in the years that lie ahead.

Thirteen lives were taken, and justice must be done
If not by judge and jury, then by a rebel's gun.

For their names will live in history, like Pearse and Lafferty,
For the freedom of our country, where all men shall be free.

## Untitled

*Anonymous (1972)*

They gave their lives for Ireland's cause,
For Irish freedom and Civil Rights laws,
For Ireland's glory they done their best,
God grant their souls eternal rest.

Rest in Peace, dear sons of freedom,
To God and Ireland you were true.
We will honour your names forever,
While we offer our prayers for you.

## Anniversary

*Joe McGrory (1973)*

A cold day it was – the sky wept – Derry wept . . .
It was long ago, (if a year is long ago)
Sixty thousand eyes their icy vigil kept,
As Derry's pride was buried 'neath the rain and snow.

Have you ever heard the sound of rifle-shot?
Crack, crack, crack again it echoed through the square.
In panic people ran and cover sought;
But thirteen murders were committed there.

And Derry wept, and people cried, and said,
'It could have been my Jim or Chris.'
Why did they die; those youths, just recent weaned from toys?
Was there a reason or was it simply this?
England has to prove that she is mighty still –
By killing boys!

Still, ill deeds such as these beget but shame,
And those who fired the shots will often rue
The day in Derry when they sullied England's name,
And rallied thousands to the cause of Brian Boru.

# The Freedom of the City (extract)

*Brian Friel (1973)*

**Michael:** We came out the front door as we had been ordered and stood on the top step with our hands above our heads. They beamed searchlights on our faces but I could see their outlines as they crouched beside their tanks. I even heard the click of their rifle-bolts. But there was no question of their shooting. Shooting belonged to a totally different order of things. And then the Guildhall Square exploded and I knew a terrible mistake had been made. And I became very agitated, not because I was dying, but that this terrible mistake be recognised and acknowledged. My mouth kept trying to form the word mistake – mistake – mistake. And that is how I died – in disbelief, in astonishment, in shock. It was a foolish way for a man to die.

**Lily:** The moment we stepped outside the front door I knew I was going to die, instinctively, the way an animal knows. Jesus, they're going to murder me! A second of panic – no more. Because it was succeeded, overtaken, overwhelmed by a tidal wave of regret, not for myself nor my family, but that life had somehow eluded me. And now it was finished; it had all seeped away; and I had never experienced it. And in the silence before my body disintegrated in a purple convulsion, I thought I glimpsed a tiny truth: that life had eluded me because never once in my forty-three years had an experience, an event, even a small unimportant happening been isolated and assessed and articulated. And the fact that this, my last experience, was denied by this perception, this was the culmination of sorrow. In a way I died of grief.

**Skinner:** A short time after I realised we were in the mayor's parlour, I knew that a price would be exacted. And when they ordered us a second time to lay down our arms, I began to suspect what that price would be because they leave nothing to chance and because the poor are always overcharged. And as we stood on the Guildhall steps, two thoughts raced through my mind: how seriously they took us and how unpardonably casual we were about them; and that to match their seriousness would demand a total dedication, a solemnity as formal as theirs. And then everything melted and fused in a great soaring heat. And my last thought was: if you're going to decide to take them on, Adrian Casimir, you've got to mend your ways. So I died, as I lived, in defensive flippancy.

# The Year of the Sloes, For Ishi

*Paul Muldoon (1973)*

In the Moon
Of Frost in the Tepees,
There were two stars
That got free.
They yawned and stretched
To white hides,
One cutting a slit
In the wall of itself
And stepping out into the night.

In the Moon
Of the Dark Red Calf,
It had learned
To track itself
By following the dots
And dashes of its blood.
It knew the silence
Deeper
Than that of birds not singing.

In the Moon
Of the snowblind,
The other fed the fire
At its heart
With the dream of a deer
Over its shoulder.
One water would wade through another,
Shivering,
Salmon of Knowledge leap the Fall.

In the Moon
Of the Red Grass Appearing,
He discovered her
Lying under a bush.
There were patches of yellowed
Snow and ice
Where the sun had not looked.
He helped her over the Black Hills
To the Ford of the Two Friends.

In the Moon
Of the Ponies Shedding,
He practised counting coups,
Knowing it harder
To live at the edge of the earth
Than its centre.
He caught the nondescript horse
And stepped
Down onto the prairies.

In the Moon
Of Making the Fat,
He killed his first bison.
Her quick knife ran under the skin
And offered the heart
To the sky.
They had been the horizon.
She saved what they could not eat
That first evening.

In the Moon
Of the Red Cherries,
She pledged that she would stay
So long as there would be
The Two-Legged

And the Four-Legged Ones,
Long as grass would grow and water
Flow, and the wind blow.
None of these things had forgotten.

In the Moon
Of the Black Cherries,
While he was looking for a place
To winter,
He discovered two wagons
Lying side by side
That tried to be a ring.
There were others in blue shirts
Felling trees for a square.

In the Moon
When the Calf Grows Hair,
There was a speck in the sky
Where he had left the tepee.
An eagle had started
Out of her side
And was waiting to return.
The fire was not cold,
The feet of six horses not circles.

In the Moon
Of the Season Changing,
He left the river
Swollen with rain.
He kicked sand over the fire.
He prepared his breast
By an ochre
That none would see his blood.
Any day now would be good to die.

In the Moon
Of the Leaves Falling,
I had just taken a bite out of the
Moon and pushed the plate
Of the world away.
Someone was asking for six troopers
Who had lain down
One after another
To drink a shrieking river.

# Derry

*Mary J Devlin (1974)*

The calmness of the city
Like impending doom,
Settles on
The deserted streets,
Passages of dust and paper.
Boarded windows, shattered buildings
Where no birdsong or creature
Can be heard –
The sadness of it all
Compels not tears,
For the broken hearts
And wasted lives,
Have long since been buried
In the debris of the
Passing years.
The writing on the wall
Will be their epitaph –
There is no tombstone big enough
To tell their tale.

# Casualty

*Seamus Heaney (1979)*

I

He would drink by himself
And raise a weathered thumb
Towards the high shelf,
Calling another rum
And blackcurrant, without
Having to raise his voice,
Or order a quick stout
By a lifting of the eyes
And a discreet dumb-show
Of pulling off the top;
At closing time would go
In waders and peaked cap
Into the showery dark,
A dole-kept breadwinner
But a natural for work.
I loved his whole manner,
Sure-footed but too sly,
His deadpan sidling tact,
His fisherman's quick eye
And turned observant back.
Incomprehensible
To him, my other life.
Sometimes on the high stool,
Too busy with his knife
At a tobacco plug
And not meeting my eye,
In the pause after a slug
He mentioned poetry.
We would be on our own

And, always politic
And shy of condescension,
I would manage by some trick
To switch the talk to eels
Or lore of the horse and cart
Or the Provisionals.
But my tentative art
His turned back watches, too:
He was blown to bits
Out drinking in a curfew
Others obeyed, three nights
After they shot dead
The thirteen men in Derry.
PARAS THIRTEEN, the walls said,
BOGSIDE NIL. That Wednesday
Everyone held
His breath and trembled.

II

It was a day of cold
Raw silence, wind-blown
Surplice and soutane:
Rained-on, flower-laden
Coffin after coffin
Seemed to float from the door
Of the packed cathedral
Like blossoms on slow water.
The common funeral
Unrolled its swaddling band,
Lapping, tightening
Till we were braced and bound
Like brothers in a ring.
But he would not be held
At home by his own crowd

Whatever threats were phoned,
Whatever black flags waved.
I see him as he turned
In that bombed offending place,
Remorse fused with terror
In his still knowable face,
His cornered outfaced stare
Blinding in the flash.
He had gone miles away
For he drank like a fish
Nightly, naturally
Swimming towards the lure
Of warm lit-up places,
The blurred mesh and murmur
Drifting among glasses
In the gregarious smoke.
How culpable was he
That last night when he broke
Our tribe's complicity?
'Now, you're supposed to be
An educated man,'
I hear him say. 'Puzzle me
The right answer to that one.'

### III

I missed his funeral,
Those quiet walkers
And sideways talkers
Shoaling out of his lane
To the respectable
Purring of the hearse . . .
They move in equal pace
With the habitual
Slow consolation

Of a dawdling engine,
The line lifted, hand
Over fist, cold sunshine
On the water, the land
Banked under fog: that morning
I was taken in his boat,
The screw purling, turning
Indolent fathoms white,
I tasted freedom with him.
To get out early, haul
Steadily off the bottom,
Dispraise the catch, and smile
As you find a rhythm
Working you, slow mile by mile,
Into your proper haunt
Somewhere, well out, beyond . . .
Dawn-sniffing revenant,
Plodder through midnight rain,
Question me again.

# Bloody Sunday

*Hugh Gallagher (1982)*

That winter came slowly to the valley
Around the River Foyle
A January sun shone on a Creggan hilltop
Thousands upon thousands gathered there
Our spirits high
Some shivered
Other stamped their feet, anxious
To be on their way
For fate awaited us, down there
Somewhere in that beautiful valley
At the end of a winding, tiring march.

Rumours, frightening stories
Spread through the gathered masses
'I seen the Saracens, extra troops . . .
Paratroopers. Red berets, hate in their eyes.'
'Wise up! Wise up! You'll scare the wains
Nothing will happen. Sure there's too many here.'

The column moved off swiftly in the end
Well past starting time . . . Derry time
Plunging down Southway, heading to the town
Strangers marvelled at the view
'Where are we going?' someone asked
'The Guildhall, the Diamond. Does anyone know?'
Blindly onward we marched
Gathering more along the way
'There's comfort in numbers,' an old woman said.

Destination unreached, confusion reigns
Fate showed its hand
Shots pierce the air
In the gathering gloom
Then screaming, shouting
More gunfire, closer now
'Run, run. As fast as you can. They've run amok!'
'What's wrong?'

# Bloody Sunday

*Hugh Gallagher (1982)*

On the day of the funerals all Ireland mourned
For the dead sons of Derry
So cruelly slain.
And they came up from Dublin, the gombeen men
In their chauffeur-driven swanky cars,
Interlopers, standing idly by beside a row of coffins
While the real mourners gathered, heads bowed,
Outside the Creggan chapel
In the howling wind and freezing rain.

Bloody, Bloody Sunday
Why did you have to happen here?
Why did our streets run red
With young innocent blood?
Why did bloodthirsty Paratroopers
Drive us from these streets
In a hail of murderous gunfire?
Was it to satisfy England's need
To deal with the bloody Irish
Who dared demand Civil Rights and freedom?

And what of the politicians and officers
Who planned this terrible day,
Skulking behind their net-curtained windows?
Jobs in the city, promotion is their fate,
While fourteen lay dead in early Derry graves
And they tell us to forget
For they have forgotten, long since,
Those apologists for British murderers.
They beat their breasts and preach of peace,
But Derry will never forget, nor forgive.

# Counting the Dead on the Radio

*Thomas McCarthy (1984)*

### I

All that winter we lined and limed the earth.
We read books, too, and ordered even more –
History rested on the brown hall table
beside the bird-guides and seed catalogues.
We read books as hungrily as Edmund
Burke, with more affection than any dauphiness.
Chaos in hard covers broke in upon us
with beautifully assembled themes, perfect
indices. Their authors played games with
being Irish, my father said. He should know.
Elsewhere, there were troubles that
the keenest authors couldn't deal with.
The way books had juggled nostalgia and fear
left us useless in the face of threat.
Who has been making midnight phone calls?
Who has been canvassing in the name of the dead?
My father has left for the city, running scared:
he wants no part in this. He has left
his number but says we should only trust
the News. We'll read more books, my mother said.
Fatherless, the radio has plenty to say.

### II

My brother had been hunting a rabbit at the water-
trough; we heard the muffled thuds and grunts
of its torture, its boy-inflicted wounds.
My mother brings the tea to the living room,
drawing sons from their serious porcelain books

into low air-raids across lemon juice.
Southern ears clogged by too much of this,
we can barely comprehend what the radio says –
something has happened up in the North; it has ruined
the Taoiseach's weekend. Adolescent soldiers
have gone wild. Peace shouldn't be fatal like this.
Lemon rind sticks to my mother's throat.
She throws up in an effort to understand. I say
Mama, a whole regiment has been attacked
by a Catholic priest waving a blood-stained
handkerchief. That's what the radio says.
My brother, with rabbit blood on his arm, sips tea,
puts his adolescent ear to the ill-tuned radio
whose crackles could be gunfire or a mild electric storm.
A household filled with books, a brother used to death:
my mother coughs again. We retune the wireless set.

## Sunday Stones

*L Morris (1986)*

Conkers, one, two, three
Falling from a tree
Hide the rip
And cover the bruises
TCP and long short trousers

People spoke
About
Houses, jobs and votes
Houses, jobs and votes

Three in the bed
And the wire from the mattress
Scrapes your leg
Flicking on and off the light
One wants to read,
The other wants to fight

The walking spoke
About
Houses, jobs and votes
Houses, jobs and votes

No socks; feet black as your boot
Flying down the brae
Elastoplast knees and brown plastic sandals
Big-wheeled trolleys
And rusty bike handles

The walking spoke
About
Houses, jobs and votes
Houses, jobs and votes
The crowd moved
And
The pavements broke
The pavements broke

GET INSIDE
I SEE THE SIGNS
KEEP AWAY
AND
DRAW THE BLINDS
DRAW THE BLINDS
DRAW THE BLINDS

The walking spoke
About
Houses, jobs and votes
Houses, jobs and votes
The crowd moved
And
The pavements broke
The pavements broke

Watching from the window
Stones, then bullets on a Sunday
Watching from the window
Stones, then bullets on a Sunday.

# Carthaginians (extract)

*Frank McGuinness (1988)*

**Scene Seven**

*Saturday night. They sit in a circle.*

**Dido:** Do you ever get afraid in this place?
**Greta:** What of?
**Dido:** Ghosts.
**Greta:** Do you believe in ghosts?
**Dido:** Yes. Do you?
**Greta:** Why do you think we're here?

*Silence.*

**Dido:** I'm scared shitless.

*Silence.*

I hope there are not going to be any poltergeists. I saw a film once about a poltergeist. It bit people's heads off and disembowelled them. I had to be nearly carried out of the cinema every time I saw it.
**Sarah:** How often did you see it?
**Dido:** Five times. It was brilliant.
**Hark:** You have great taste in films.
**Dido:** Yea, I know. I see everything.
**Hark:** Nothing like a good Western.
**Dido:** When you were a kid, Hark, playing Cowboys and Indians, which were you?
**Hark:** The Indian.
**Dido:** You get weirder by the minute.
**Hark:** What's wrong with Indians?
**Dido:** They always get beaten.

**Hark:** Not always.
**Seph:** I like the Indians as well. Their headdresses were great.
**Hark:** They had the best words.
**Paul:** Firewater.
**Hark:** Medicine man.
**Seph:** Peace pipe.
**Paul:** Great words. Like poetry.
**Maela:** When I was young, at school like, I quite liked poetry. I don't remember any poems. I tell a lie, I do remember one. How did it go?
*'Is there anyone there?' said the Traveller –*
**Paul:** *Knocking on the moonlit door*
**Greta:** *And his horse in the silence champed the grasses*
*Of the forest's ferny floor*
*And a bird – and a bird –*
**Sarah:** *– a bird flew up out of the turret,*
*Above the Traveller's head:*
*And he smote on the door a second time;*
*'Is there anybody there?' he said.*
**Hark:** *But no one descended to the Traveller;*
*No head from the leaf-fringed sill*
*Leaned over and looked into his grey eyes –*
**Seph:** *Where he stood –*
**Dido:** *– perplexed –*
**Paul:** *– and still.*
**Greta:** *But only a host of phantom listeners*
*That dwelt in the lone house then*
*Stood listening in the quiet of the moonlight*
*To that voice from the world of men . . .*
**Seph:** *And he felt in his heart their strangeness –*
**Paul:** *Their stillness answering his cry . . .*
*For he suddenly smote on the door, even*
*Louder, and lifted his head.*
**Sarah:** *'Tell them I came, and no one answered,*

|          | *That I kept my word,' he said.* |
| -------- | -------- |
| **Maela:** | *Never the least stir made the listeners* |
|          | *Though every word he spake –* |
| **Greta:** | *Fell echoing through the shadowiness of* |
|          | *the still house* |
|          | *From the one man left awake.* |
|          | *Aye, they heard his foot on the stirrup,* |
| **Maela:** | *And the sound of iron on stone,* |
| **Sarah:** | *And how the silence surged softly backward,* |
| **Women:** | *When the plunging hoofs were gone.* |

*Silence.*

| **Seph:** | Do you ever write poetry now, Hark? |
| -------- | -------- |
| **Hark:** | I wrote doggerel. |
| **Paul:** | Some good stuff. Heady days back then. |
| **Hark:** | You would have been only a kid, Dido. |
| **Dido:** | There were no kids after Bloody Sunday. |
| **Paul:** | Do you remember their names? The dead of Bloody Sunday? |

*Silence.*

**Paul:** Bernard McGuigan, forty-one years, Iniscarn Gardens, Derry. Patrick Doherty, thirty-two years, Hamilton Street, Derry. Michael Kelly, seventeen, from Dunmore Gardens, Derry. William McKinney, twenty-seven, from Westway, Derry. James Wray, twenty-seven, Drumcliffe Avenue, Derry. Hugh Gilmour, seventeen years old, Garvan Place, Derry. Jack Duddy, who was seventeen, Central Drive, Derry. William Nash, nineteen, Dunree Gardens, Derry. Michael McDaid, twenty-one, Tyrconnell Street, Derry. Gerald Donaghey, seventeen, Meenan Square, Derry. John Young, seventeen, Westway, Derry.

Kevin McElhinney, seventeen, Phillip Street, Derry. Gerard McKinney, Knockdara House, Waterside, Derry.

**Hark:** Perpetual light shine upon you. Rest in peace.
**Seph:** Bloody Sunday.
**Sarah:** Sunday.
**Greta:** Sunday.
**Sarah:** Sunday.
**Greta:** Wash the dead.
**Paul:** Bury the dead.
**Seph:** Sunday.
**Sarah:** Raise the dead.
**Hark:** Sunday.
**Dido:** Do you see the dead?
**Greta:** The dead beside you.
**Maela:** The dead behind you.
**Sarah:** The dead before you.
**Greta:** Forgive the dead.
**Maela:** Forgive the dying.
**Sarah:** Forgive the living.
**Paul:** Forgive yourself.
**Hark:** Forgive yourself.
**Seph:** Forgive yourself.
**Maela:** Bury the dead.
**Greta:** Raise the living.
**Sarah:** Wash the living.

*Light breaks through the graveyard.*
*Birdsong begins.*
*Light illuminates them all.*
*They listen, looking at each other, in the light.*
*They lie down and sleep.*
*It is now morning.*
*Dido is alone in the graveyard.*

**Dido:** What happened? Everything happened, nothing happened, whatever you want to believe, I suppose. What do I believe? I believe it is time to leave Derry. Love it and leave it. Now or never. Why am I talking to myself in a graveyard? Because everyone in Derry talks to themselves. Everybody in the world talks to themselves. What's the world? Shipquay Street and Ferryquay Street and Rossville Street and William Street and the Strand and Great James Street. While I walk the earth, I walk through you, the streets of Derry. If I meet one who knows you and they ask, how's Dido? Surviving. How's Derry? Surviving. Carthage has not been destroyed. Watch yourself.

*Dido drops flowers on the sleepers.*

Watch yourself, Hark and Sarah. Watch yourself, Seph. Watch yourself, Paul. Watch yourself, Greta. Watch yourself, Maela. Remember me. Watch yourself, Dido. Watch yourself, Derry. Watch yourself. Watch yourself. Watch yourself.

*Dido caresses Seph's guitar, half-covered with the tricolour.*

Play.

*Dido exits as the music plays.*

# Marchers

*Eoghan MacCormaic (1989)*

Behind a banner
the crowd is disorderly order
in the photograph.
The older experienced veterans
fewer now among the young.
A fact turned sideways in conversation,
a downward glance at a carried wreath,
a heavy coat, a headscarf, plain people,
a camera slung round a neck
idly, hopefully idle,
and capturing no more
than this reconvened mass
of the faithful who have walked
sadly, proudly, defiantly,
along this route, seventeen Sundays,
seventeen years.
And the offspring,
the children who weren't born
when that first march
made cameras click in shocked horror
as fourteen fathers, brothers, sons,
were slain.
And thousands survived the ambush
on these streets,
remembered today and always
by the marchers.

## Obráid Domhnach Na Fola

*Dan Baron Cohen / Derry Frontline (1991)*

Fiche bliain ó shin inniu,
Nuair a briseadh agóid an phobail,
Ag ghuth saibhir lucht na úsáide,
i bpostaeirí faoi chois agus brógaí fuilsmeartha,
Rinneadh lúbra scanraithe dár sráideanna,
Obráid Dhomhnach na Fola á comhlíonadh.

Fiche bliain ó shin inniu,
Nuair a bhrúigh guth maoineachais an dúshaothraithe,
Aisling na ndaoine
Taobh thiar de bhallaí an anba agus doirsi dochta na heagla,
Cuireadh faoi ghlas tí muintir Dhoire,
Obráid Dhomhnach na Fola á comhlíonadh.

Fiche bliain ó shin inniu,
Nuair a shocraigh guth brúidiúil dlí agus reachta,
Go marófar pobal soineanta,
Ceithre uair déag i ndiaidh a chéile in aon lá amháin,
Tiontaíodh Éire ina mharbhlann tostach,
Obráid Dhomhnach na Fola á comhlíonadh.

Fiche bliain ó shin inniu,
Nuair a ghluais muintir Dhoire in éadan imthreorannú,
Bhí mé dhá bhliain déag d'aois,
Agus cé nach gcuimhním ar shagart an chiarsúir póca,
Tá ceithre cholm déag á n-íompar agam agus beart agam iad a úsáid,
Mar fhianaíse ar Obráid Dhomhnach na Fola.

Inniu nuair a iarrann muid ár gcearta,
Is guth milliúin dá leithéid coir,
Osclaímis ár gcoilm,
Ina súil dhúchais agus ina aibhneacha saoirse,
Go ngluaiseadh Doire ina sruth fríd sráídeanna gáire,
Ar aghaidh chun todhchaí saor ó Dhommhnach na Fola eíle.

## Operation Bloody Sunday

*Dan Baron Cohen / Derry Frontline (1991)*

Twenty years ago today
When the well-heeled voice of exploitation
Scattered a people's protest
Into trampled placards and bloodstained shoes
Our streets were turned into mazes of terror
Operation Bloody Sunday fulfilled.

Twenty years ago today
When the sterling voice of occupation
Drove a people's vision
Behind walls of panic and locked doors of fear
Derry was placed under house arrest
Operation Bloody Sunday fulfilled.

Twenty years ago today
When the brutal voice of law and order
Decided an innocent people
Be murdered fourteen times in one day
Ireland was turned into a silent morgue
Operation Bloody Sunday fulfilled.

Twenty years ago today
When Derry marched against Internment
I was just two years old
And though I don't remember the handkerchief priest
I carry fourteen scars and I plan to use them
As evidence of Operation Bloody Sunday.

Today when we call for justice
With the voice of a million such crimes
Let us open our scars
Into eyes of hope and rivers of freedom
So that Derry might flow through laughing streets
Into a future of no more bloody Sundays.

# Let the Stones Speak

*Emmylou Large (1992)*

My Bloody Sunday

'I'd been there from the start,
I'd seen it all
An insignificant piece of stone.
Laid by the masons to form a gable wall.
The gable wall of number one Lecky Road
Now standing alone, ghostly white,
Showing only bold black lettering
Splattered with paint bombs.
A house no longer, just a wall.
I knew there was trouble in the air.
The shifty look of the troopers
With sleek black gun barrels glinting in the light.

Suddenly . . . CHAOS!

Round after round of ammunition,
From scarlet-topped camouflaged blurs
Leaving a trail of crimson,
Showing no mercy.
Screams of plea left them still,
Showing no remorse.
They shot on . . .
Disembedded from my friends,
By a stray lead bullet,
I know, aimed at an innocent one.
Barely time to hit the ground, but held aloft,
By a tear-stained, scruffy boy,
Shouting obscenities at those willing to listen.
He hurls me through the air,

Until I clash with camouflage, green, bullet-proof steel
The blow is severe as once again I fall to the ground.

I'm stained now, with the blood on which I fell.
Of one of thirteen innocents who lay here before.
Half of me dripping with the colour of a beret,
The beret of a man,
Who smothers me with a heavy, leather-coated pair
And once again I rocket into flight.

Only a pawn in a battle between the law
And the innocent.'

# Sunday, Bloody Sunday

*Tommy Sands (1992)*

They were walking, they were talking, they were laughing, they were singing,
Calling out for Civil Rights and freedom,
And peace was on the banner that was blowing in the breeze,
All upon that Sunday, Bloody Sunday.

Some were chatting with their lovers, some were walking holding hands,
Some were dreaming of a greater future dawning,
But who could tell that darkness would descend upon their dreams,
All upon that Sunday, Bloody Sunday.

Screaming, then a burst of blood, 'Oh, Jesus!' someone cried,
A lad of seventeen is lying dying,
And thirteen more would follow him before the day would end,
Oh cursed be that Sunday, Bloody Sunday.

They were walking, they were talking, they were laughing, they were singing,
And calling out for Civil Rights and freedom,
But now it was a flag of blood that fluttered in the breeze,
A curse upon that Sunday, Bloody Sunday.

## Bloody Sunday Revisited

*Anonymous (1992)*

'Too long a sacrifice
Can make a stone of the heart.
O when may it suffice?'
**WB Yeats**

A small man in combat clothes
lowered his gun to his hip
and sprayed like a tomcat
the lethal ballistics of territory:
sovereignty asserted by the injection of bullets
into puzzled chests and stomachs
surprised faces and fragile skulls
of those who only live here.

Two decades later, I listen
look mostly in vain
for signs
that the wounds of the dead
heal
that children are not born
with stigmata
of those old bullet wounds.

Many would not talk
for fear
of bursting the scars
or fear of weeping
or that I
would put them on TV
or twist their words
to prove something.

I move from home to bereaved home
as priests did
on that Mass funeral day
taking time in between
to ease
the abiding weight of their words
the slabs of fourteen gravestones
that have crushed these hearts.

# Remembering Bloody Sunday

*Paul Laughlin (1994)*

In each day's journey
To work or to school
We retrace the steps of the dead.
Behind small routines
We are mindful
Of what has been:
And if innocence has fled
Their screams
Will not leave this place
While that offence remains.

# Looking Back to the Future

*Jackie Duddy (1995)*

As I stand here looking over Derry
I'm amazed at the changes I see in just twenty-four years.
When I think of the small community I left,
The little houses where families of fifteen lived, ate and
slept together.
The little shops where everyone got their groceries,
The streets of houses where every front door was open in
the morning
And stayed open until night,
The children playing outside, the friends,
Everyone knew everyone by name,
Just like one big happy family.

I'm confused and puzzled at what I see now.
People passing people without even saying hello,
The roads so full of traffic, cars, buses, lorries.
Everyone working hard so they can live in bigger houses,
Have bigger cars, more money,
I wonder would I have liked all this?
The town has grown so big and so far out,
Shopping centres like something out of space in my eyes.
I'm amazed at it all.

But, I don't know if I would have liked it,
Don't know what would have been in store for me.
Would I have been a boxing champion? My boyhood dream?
Would I have married and had children of my own?
Would I have been a businessman or maybe on the dole?
I'll never know, because I was killed at the age of seventeen,
Not given the chance of making a life for myself,
Not given the choice.

Maybe I should have stayed at home that day,
Maybe I should not have marched for justice,
Maybe I'm better off in the beautiful place I'm in now,
Just maybe.

# William Nash

*Amanda C Rowe (1995)*

Just a name, William Nash
Just an age, nineteen years
Just another victim of violence.

William Nash, with his well-
groomed hair, his fresh new suit.
Marching for the internees,
Marching for what could have been him or his family.

Along with another ten thousand.
Why did it have to be him?

An outstanding boy with
a future of happiness, fulfilment.

It was said he was shot running away.
Running away, running away,
And the Para will always say, 'I was shooting in defence,
I was personally confronted with an armed man.'

His father running to the defenceless body
of his unarmed son laying helpless,
suffering and yet left alone.

Alexander, shot trying to comfort his dying son.
And they say it wasn't premeditated!

As the saying goes 'one for all and all for one'.
WIDGERY ENGLISH GOVERNMENT?!
(RING ANY BELLS?!)

**Minds Locked Shut**

*Christy Moore (1996)*

It happened on a Sunday afternoon,
On a lovely bright winter's afternoon,
On a perfect day,
On a perfect day for walking.

There were gunshots, stones and bullets
On a lovely bright winter's afternoon.
There was chaos, panic and death,
Disbelief upon the faces,
Fear and bewilderment.

Seconds seem so long,
They're firing bullets at us,
It was not supposed to be like this,
Awesome to behold.

And then our minds locked shut.
And then our minds locked shut.
And then our minds locked shut.
And then our minds locked shut.

And there remains . . .

Jackie Duddy  Willie Nash
Gerry Donaghey  Willie McKinney
Gerard McKinney  Jim Wray
Johnny Johnston  Barney McGuigan
Paddy Doherty  Kevin McElhinney
John Young  Mickey Kelly
Hugh Gilmour  Michael McDaid

Let us remember

It happened on a Sunday afternoon,
On a lovely bright winter's afternoon,
On a perfect day,
On a perfect day for walking.

# I Wasn't Even Born

*Sharon Meenan and Killian Mullan (1997)*

I remember people happy and the confidence of that morning.
The Creggan Shops.
I remember the banner that was carried. The gathered message.
I remember live fire.
A pool of blood on the pavement.
I remember Hugh Gilmour and Patrick Doherty.
I remember running. The Flats.
I remember Jim Wray and Michael McDaid.
I remember screaming.
English accents.
I remember William Nash and Gerald McKinney.
I remember a crazed army.
A white hanky.
I remember Michael Kelly and John Young.
I remember it black and white. But blood is always red.
I remember Jackie Duddy and Bernard McGuigan.
I remember looking for my friend from the confusion and then through the quiet.
I remember Gerald Donaghey and Kevin McElhinney.
I remember hearing the news.
I remember John Johnston and William McKinney.
I remember thirteen coffins. Black flags.
I remember a young woman with an old face.
The funerals.
I remember my father crying hot angry tears.
I remember the lies.
And I wasn't even born.

# Running Uphill

*Declan McLaughlin (1997)*

How many times must we do this to ourselves?
Been on our knees a million times, asking for your help.
Of all the answers that I don't understand,
Like I did not draw the firing line but still to know where to stand.
Nobody told me, must have heard it on the news,
People with nothing still had everything to lose.

It's like running uphill.
It's like running uphill.

In the corner of a graveyard a mother kneels to pray,
In the memory of a son that slowly fades away.
And in this part of the graveyard the sun no longer shines,
There's no fences or barbed-wire, but still she's doing time.
Until she gets the answers to the questions that she asks
It's hard to build a future when you're haunted by the past.

It's like running uphill.
It's like running uphill.

As the bodies hit the pavement,
The world seen what you done.
As the bodies hit the pavement,
Somebody's singing that We Will Overcome!

It's like running uphill.
It's like running uphill.

And everybody gathered here in Central Drive
Is marching in the shadows of the truth you tried to hide.
And every step that's taken is a breaking of your law,
For your justice never added up to the murder that we saw.
And time don't make no difference
To the people that still care.
In thousands we march the streets
Still knowing that you're there.

It's like running uphill.
It's like running uphill.

# Injustice

*John F McCartney (1998)*

Crowd mingling cacophony
Rhapsody of spirit in sympathy;
Stifled groans, high-velocity hornets,
Wanging wasps, airborne jets
Of death, from black melting faces;
Pitiless, in this heartless oasis.

Crumpled corpses lie grotesquely,
Shocked stalwarts, shuffling quietly;
Silence strutting the stillness softly,
Sudden hot bouncing tracers echoing loftily;
White flag fluttering, despairing,
Trembling eyes, shaking hands, caring.

From the flaming ashes of this injustice
Will rise our phoenix, trust us;
Not now, perhaps, but unforgettable,
Minds burned with scenes indelible;
Streets cry, this outrage shall not pass,
No more, no more, no more second class.

## The Grief of Derry

*Jackie Duddy (1998)*

It happened on a Sunday afternoon,
Thirteen of Derry's sons were taken
Despite their cries.
Plucked from the crowd at random.
Removed from family and friends they loved,
To cold unknown surroundings.

That day began like any other,
Yet ended in despair,
Some say a mystery, some say planned,
No consolation to the grieving families,
Whose wounds still smart from the injustice,
Whose hearts still grieve, longing for that last goodbye,
And the reason, WHY?

# Tribute to Lord Fenner-Brockway
*John Dunne (1999)*

Fumbling friendly hands
Gently smuggled you,
A frail old man
To speak on their behalf,
Onto the back of an old battered lorry
Drawn up against
Caker Casey's Free Derry Wall.
You meant to speak
Against injustice
Borne too long
By people prepared to take no more.

The dumb microphone beckoned.
The unwitting signal, now it seems
To send the bullets flying,
Murderous music – a dance of death
Choreographed by pitiless politicians
Too afraid of what you might have had to say.

The cruelty implicit in that first clear crisp
Flesh-rending rifle crack
Still numbs my shattered soul.
Momentary disbelief evaporated
And crabs went scuttling-scared
Shielded only by Bernadette's
Uselessly defiant protestations
'Stand your ground,
They cannot shoot us all.'

And then I saw the black walls
Menacing,

Threatening,
Chillingly forbidding –
And I sought safety
Scrambling with my friends,
Oblivious to the silent screams
Of spirit – witnesses strangely garbed.
Massacred, at other times,
In other lands,
Standing steeped again
In innocent blood
On Derry's hallowed ground.
Pointing.

'Admit your guilt;
Seek forgiveness
And reconciliation is assured.'
The wish of innocence – true,
Lord Saville – now – it's up to you.

## That Fateful Day

*Martin Wray (1999)*

'Our sons are dead,' the women say,
Some have come to kneel and pray,
A carnival mood around our town,
By four o'clock thirteen gunned down.

The shooting starts.
Bang, bang, all around the bullets fly,
And on Derry's streets our men did die.

All bodies now identified and claimed,
These murdering soldiers should be ashamed,
A march for peace, that's all it was,
Did so many families deserve this loss?

Now friends and family have gathered round,
The silence is deafening, there isn't a sound,
Our home begins to fill with tears,
With the confirmation of our fears,
'He's gone, you know,' my father said,
I just can't believe my brother's dead.

And then the funerals come.
Thirteen coffins side by side,
It was in this town they lived and died,
And in the cemetery I can't get near,
To say goodbye to the one I loved dear.

A march for peace that ends in murder.
Those men have done a callous deed,
Was there ever really any need?
And then the so-called inquiry begins,
It only exonerates them from their sins.

Even as time goes by I don't forget,
Though sometimes I feel as if we never met,
It was so quick and very sudden.
And to this day they have the nerve,
To refuse us the justice we all deserve.

A march for 'peace', so why did they die?

# A Disarming Suggestion

*Perry McDaid (1999)*

The corner chosen as a refuge
Stank of excrement, blood and death,
For wild-eyed rabid Paras
Had shot them where they cowered
Unarmed, soiling trousers
Pressed neatly by proud wives and mothers.

Words bubbled from their
Lacerated lungs, mingling with mucus and blood
Which steamed indignant in its innocence
As, for good measure, the possessed
Swung vicious stocks.

Recalled by frantic falsetto,
Grinning gruesome in their hysteria,
Seasoned soldiers stared deadly
At chilling corpses;
Private thoughts cloaked, automatons
Edged silently from the niche
To emerge amid a swarm of horror.

A priest was waving a tear-stained handkerchief,
One pitiful flag of truce,
As grown men – shaking in shock and fear –
Fumbled limp figures from line of fire;
And CS gas shrouded the fallen.

Oh yes, decommission;
The defenceless are easier targets.

# They Were Better Than Most

*Paddy McCourt (2000)*

Although I wasn't born on that day,
Together we all remember Bloody Sunday.
In nineteen eighty-three I was born,
But back in seventy-two, the people's hearts were torn.
But we all stand here in the rain,
You can almost feel the people's pain.
Together we all stand here hand-in-hand,
There's a sense of sadness throughout the land.
For the families they've lost someone close,
They were greater than them, they were better than most.
So please, poor children, wipe your tears,
This land is changing, there is no fear.
Let us hope and let us pray,
That those poor people will have their day.
Let us hope and let us pray,
That those who done it will be caught one day.

# Uncle Jackie

*Paul Campbell (2001)*

Here's a story about a boy whose life was rich 'til he was robbed of it,
he had a loving mother who passed on but a loving father who still stood strong,
five brothers and nine sisters, all of whom loved him truly,
then one day he went on a march even though his father had told him not to.

'It's only a Civil Rights march,' is what he called to his debating sisters,
'but Daddy told us not to,' is what they had said but he was still in bed,
so off he ran to meet John Young, they were going on that march to have some fun,
things were going fine 'til the soldiers came, then throwing began in freedom's name.

'Why won't they let us march? It's Civil Rights, why can't they see this?
We didn't want any trouble from you so why do you have to interfere here?'
So the bullets were fired, the riots begun so they decided to run,
'Come on, John,' said Jackie, 'we'd better be gone because this ain't no fun.'

One last laugh as he saw that Father Daly had overtaken him,
and as he laughed that last laugh – his life was ended with a single blast,
up the street came Aunt Dolly with the dreaded news of that day,
'I'm so sorry, Willie, but young Jackie's been killed today.'

# No Longer Cry

*Robert McDaid and Patrick O'Doherty (2001)*

Like Martin's folk down Georgia way,
People marched on the road that day,
A carnival as they all set out
They would be heard, there was no doubt.

Missiles rainin' higher 'n' higher,
Stinging gas, rubber then Live Fire
Runnin' for the high flats 'n' hope,
Some fell by the sniper's scope.

Blood on the rubble, terror in the square,
Hit in the back, long flaying hair,
No mercy for a white coat, cleric or flag,
Another one down as they boast and brag.

Broken bodies on a cold morgue floor,
They laughed 'n' joked as they kept the score,
Father searching for a missing son,
Humiliation at the point of a gun.

What could've been for you 'n' me,
Heaven knows we'll never see,
Lookin' forward to the future we faced,
What a pity, such a waste.

Thinkin' back I can no longer cry,
No more tears, the well has run dry,
Endless circles for a reason why,
We didn't even get to say goodbye.

# Pablo's Part

*Julieann Campbell (2001)*

Riot scene, feign fury for the army
Rubber bricks and polystyrene barricades
A camaraderie of sorts. Until the big scene.

Overwhelmed, he hid his anxiety well
Actually acted out that fabled family tale.
He quietly complied –
Becoming someone else, for just a while.
His false bravado not fooling anyone.

Hours later, as we nursed our well-earned drinks,
I wiped a touch of grime from his collar, without thinking –
And glimpsing remnants of the fake blood – he quietly caved in.
Swiftly broken, let the façade fall.

# The Story of Bloody Sunday in Verse (extract)

*JP McMenamin (2001)*

Then one by one the coffins
Oh, Lord with me abide
Laid to rest in Creggan
The very angels cried.

Rain fell on Derry city
As the coffins one by one
Were lowered into the cold dark earth
Fathers, brothers – sons.

Of the thirteen who were murdered
By the soldiers of the Queen
Six were merely children
Their age? Just seventeen.

Thirteen coffins lie together
Horrors hide beneath the veneer
Polished oak obscures the slaughter
Polished handles – burnished tears.

Death is awful, death is ugly
Hid away, kept out of sight
Packaged up in tiny boxes
Death is fearsome – like the night.

Up above, the sound of rotors
Helicopters overhead
Cameras pointing at the mourners
Vultures circling o'er the dead.

And yet, even at the funeral
Still not equal – second class
Locked out in the pouring rain
No room for them at Mass.

Admission, ticket only
Just like a football match
Up front sit politicians
Those outside can only watch.

But then it's always been the same
The poor are cast aside
To make way for politicians
TV coverage, worldwide.

Where were they on that Sunday
When the people gave their life?
Listen to their pious statements
As they warn of civil strife.

And still the rain kept falling
The graveyard turned to mud
But if it rained forever
It could never wash away the blood.

The heavy earth is shovelled in
The coffins disappear
Daddy won't be home tonight
A young child sheds a tear.

Back then to the little homes
Which have been torn apart
A change of clothes, a cup of tea
Will it mend a broken heart?

And still the rain kept falling
Tears for those who died
The rain fell straight from heaven
The very angels cried.

# Muted Martyrs

*Perry McDaid (2001)*

An obelisk marks their passing;
in a pool of blood-red wreaths
it stands motionless, unassuming,
blending into the concrete foliage
of paving, steps, and first-storey terrace.

People bustle by,
intent upon meaningless chores;
memories of that fateful day faint,
swamped by a deluge of atrocity –
buried beneath the debris of ferocity,
the idiocy of those who will have no compromise.
No real surprise.

So sorrow and outrage lie dormant
until the next anniversary,
or when some callous adversary
tries to deny the truth.

Loyalists, Royalists bemoan
imagined oppression, rage indignant
of loss of rights. Blights,
these silver-spoon sucklings know nothing
of injustice and, while they pout and cry,
the ones who dream of equality die;

and all the while an endless cycle
spins, washing old tragedies away
with a rinse of new sorrows –
and each who forget Bloody Sunday cede.

An obelisk marks their passing;
nothing changes amidst the ubiquitous lip-flapping.

# One Sunday

*Gerry Dorrity (2001)*

One Sunday I went walking with my Daddy and his Dad.
I didn't understand why everyone was looking so sad.
I asked my Da the reason, and this is what he said.

'These people here are marching, son, to commemorate the day
That the British Army came to town and took thirteen lives away.

Nearly thirty years ago, the feelings were so strong.
That people took to the streets; they felt that things were wrong.
Decent jobs and houses and the right to vote.
The Civil Rights leaders were calling from the back of their float.

The banter was freely flowing, yet there was tension in the air,
As we tried to make our way onto the Guildhall Square.
The Brits put up a barricade, they said we're not allowed.
We started to get angry; soon a few became a crowd.

We'd come too far this day, to turn and just go home.
So some stayed on to hurl abuse and some were hurling stones.
An end to Internment, we called and give us Civil Rights.
We didn't really expect the Brits to put up that kind of fight.

We always ignored the rubber bullets and the CS gas.
Bur they must have meant business when they called in the Paras.
The piercing shrill of live rounds sent panic through the streets.
As I looked around me, I saw bodies at my feet.

I ran for my protection and saw blood upon my shirt,
When I tried to help a man who I saw was badly hurt.
His face will always haunt me, that day I won't forget.
For those wounds are still open, we haven't healed them yet.

We buried fourteen bodies, they buried the truth.
But now there's this enquiry, if that is any use.
I'll be interested to hear what they offer as an excuse.'

So on Monday I am going for a walk with my Daddy and his Dad.
We'll walk beyond the Guildhall Square.
I want to see what happens, I hope it turns out fair.

# 1 Para

*Scott MX Turner (2002)*

Derry, Ireland, seventy-two, and Nationalists are on the move
In the streets, on the job, in the schools
Irish people use all the tools
Late January a crisp bright day
people mass in Creggan to say
'End Internment Now' – but the British Army had other ideas
The NICRA march was banned
you know what kind of plan bans demands
for Civil Rights, for fair housing
for the right to vote, the right to hope
that you ain't caught in the scope on a sniper's rifle
SLR follow you down

The truth shot down will rise again
The truth shot down will rise

You gotta understand for the British
this had nothing to do with public order
with keeping the peace, with making society safe and sound
This was an operation to take control
to roll, to flash-attack
to take back the Bogside
a No-Go zone liberated by the people who live there
So live ammo was the plan
Snipers in derelict houses under the Derry Walls
calls roar through transceiver sets in the soldiers' ears
secure channel
Lies just fly when a cover-up covers up murder
There in the Bogside by the Rossville Flats
just like that, it was the victims who were blamed

The truth shot down will rise again
The truth shot down will rise

It was the British Information Service
served us more lies
they tried to say that there were gunshots
that there were nail bombs
that there was petrol
that there were mobs and throngs of Irish
and it was 1 Para that was on the defensive
they had to discharge weapons to stay alive
or so they say
It was a No-Go zone
well there's Wilford on the phone
he's proud he says he owns the Bogside
He's finally occupied the Bogside
and it was worth every Taig's blood spilled
by the Rossville Flats
Lord Widgery, what a travesty
told 'move it off the front page'
never mind the rage
as the days turn to months turn to years
tears as the years turn to lifetimes lost
Someday they may say in the UK
with straight face that they were sorry
But no Para will ever stand trial
So the real tribunals are the funerals
the Masses, fourteen times, fourteen crimes
We may hear why the Paras opened fire
on the people they want behind the wire
There were orders to keep the order
didn't matter how but it matters now
with the truth shot down this town
will never be free

'til like a phoenix it rises up
and it spreads its wings
and we sing a song, a soldier's song
we sing it strong
at the Free Derry Corner

The truth shot down will rise again
The truth shot down will rise.

## William Street, Derry, January 2002
## (After Yeats et al)

*Berni Kerr (2002)*

By corners where the Martyrs fell,
Words neither Meaningless nor Polite,
Are snarled and slurred, while Ireland's Youth,
Prepare to Fight the Ancient Fight.

Where blood was shed for Ireland's sake,
And Liberty her last stand took,
Cathleen Ní Houlihan, in high heels,
Trails Heaven's Cloths through pools of puke.

The Poor Old Woman calls her sons,
To win again her Fourth Green Field,
But Cuchullan in the taxi rank
Has made his Stand, and will not Yield.

Gone are the clouds of CS gas,
The petrol bombs we took for stars,
Only the bullet holes remain,
Unhealed and still unhealing scars.

Yet sweet is the sleep the Heroes sleep,
Who walk no more down Creggan's hill,
To William Street where, row on row,
Wait ghosts of Paras, grinning, still.

## My Role Was That of an Observer (General Robert Ford)

*Mary O'Malley (2002)*

Your blue eyes, Danny boy,
Your black hair.
They were all armed, the men. Marching!
And that shape there is . . .
Very like a gun.
No, more like a nail bomb, forsooth.
Yes, your honour, very like a nail bomb.
More like a widget, methinks, m'lord. Yes
Very like a widget, so we shot it.
Widgety Lord Widgery. Thirteen widgets
Weapon carriers, every seventeen-year-old
Fenian one of them, Sir.
It was a Sunday. There was snow.
Thirty years ago. Seventeen
the age to love, the year to die.
Your dark hair, Danny boy,
Your blue terrorist eyes.

## Monday, 31 January 1972

*Tony Ramsay (2002)*

'There'll be no school today, son,'
Said the lady as she tightened
The double knot of her blue headscarf
Tucking it well in beneath her chin
Into the buttoned-up neckline
Of her winter coat.
We stood before the locked gates
Of the Christian Brothers, Brow of the Hill,
On Lecky Road.

So back, along Deanery Street
Through Bluebell Hill Gardens
Across the College Field
Up, through the cemetery
And home to Cromore Gardens.
All day my mother stopped
Whatever she was doing
To turn up the radio
When the news came on.

There were thirteen dead.

Patrick Doherty – Thirty-one
Dead.

Gerald Donaghey – Seventeen
Dead.

Jackie Duddy – Seventeen
Dead.

Hugh Gilmour – Seventeen
Dead.

Michael Kelly – Seventeen
Dead.

Michael McDaid – Twenty
Dead.

Kevin McElhinney – Seventeen
Dead.

Bernard McGuigan – Forty-one
Dead.

Gerard McKinney – Thirty-four
Dead.

William McKinney – Twenty-seven
Dead.

William Nash – Nineteen
Dead.

James Wray – Twenty-two
Dead.

John Young – Seventeen
Dead.

I was nine. I remember

Prayers and tears and silence
Around a large dark pool of congealed blood
On a pavement at the Rossville Flats.

Hushed tones and tears piercing
The dark and silence at the front door
Of Duddy's house on Central Drive.

And on Tuesday, in our chapel, more
Coffins and more grief and more tears
And more silence
Than I had ever seen.

And the rain, on Wednesday,
Cold and driven.

Thirteen dead.
All of us wounded.

I can still smell the silence –
Still taste the reverent disbelief
On the back of my throat.

# Scenes From an Inquiry (extract)

*Dave Duggan (2002)*

**Scene Seven – A Bestiary**

**Counsel:** Surely you can't ask us to believe you saw a . . . a . . . gorgon?

**Witness:** Lots of them. Belching fire. And fury. And five-headed mastiffs, big as jet bombers. I still see them. Cerberus out front, so awful that when he came towards us we all froze. He spat at us and poison burned the air.

**Counsel:** My Lord, these are myths.

**Witness:** And Balor strode among us that day, put the evil eye on all of us. Took the breath of all of us. Took the life of some of us. Ravaged our heels. Scattered us, a herd of red deer flying over the hillside, our feet dragging and sluggish in the heather of our fear.

**Counsel:** My Lord, I must ask you . . .

**Witness:** Centaurs trampled the streets, hurling bolts of lightning. Werewolves big as aircraft carriers slabbered over us. Eagles clawed at our hair and at our skin. I saw a woman fall and be lifted up and tossed away by a mastodon. I see her still.

**Judge:** If I may? Counsel has already referred to your nineteen seventy-two statement in which you mention Basilisks. Would you care to . . .

**Witness:** All they have to do is look at you. They came in armoured vehicles and got down on one knee, half bird, with luminous feathers, half reptile, with gangrenous scales. And they looked at us. 'Don't look back,' I shouted, but some did and they were felled by the glares.

**Counsel:** I mean, how can we ever get to the truth of this?

**Judge**: We have to accept the language we're given. I mean we talk about "pigs", don't we?

**Witness:** There were pigs, wild boars. Grunting, snorting and roaring over the waste ground towards the flats.

**Counsel:** At last, something we can deal with. Waste ground. Can I ask you to look at this photograph please?

## Herm
(In memory of Ted Hughes)

*Paul Muldoon (2002)*

He stands in under the hedge, among the sweet-smelling flags,
and holds out a white flag
to the distant plow-team
that makes directly for him through the teem

of rain, his head one of those plastered, round stones
atop a heap of pavers and kidney stones.
Or he might be a young holly or ash
what with the brow-beat of ash.

As the team bears down on him through the fertile
meadow, the white on the lead horse's forehead (like the
white where a tile
once fell off the wall behind the range)
comes into range

and a priest with a handkerchief
reels among those mown down in Derry, whispering to him,
'Chief . . .'
as he grips his wrist and starts counting,
'We were counting

on you to hold steady, to stay
our consolation and stay.'
'But I've always taken my bearings from you,' he'll hear
himself remark,
'it was you I took for my mark.'

## Maire – A Woman of Derry (extract)

*Brian Foster (2002)*

His white shirt was spattered red with blood. Not his blood. The blood of others.

He burst through the front door and cowered in the hallway like a terrified hunted animal . . .

Hands shakin'. Eyes bulgin'. Face deathly white.

It took ages. But eventually he told me his story.

(*Here she stands up and faces directly out into the audience as she repeats word for word Tommy's account of what happened.*)

It all started out so peaceful, Maire. So relaxed. Almost carnival-like.

Twenty thousand people. Men women and children in their Sunday finest they'd worn to Mass earlier. Long-haired youths in parka jackets. Factory girls linkin' arms. Heads uncovered. Singin' songs.

As me 'n' Andy reach the Bishop's Field, they're just settin' off down the hill towards the Bogside. A lorry leads the way. On it a big Civil Rights Association banner flutters in the breeze.

All around us . . . shouts . . . squeals . . . laughter . . . bubblin' up like . . . well, like a fountain of optimism.

Overhead . . . even the sun smiles down its approval on us.

A rousing chorus of *We Shall Overcome* breaks out. Me 'n' Andy join in. Great craic.

Young lovers stroll hand-in-hand.

A father carries his son on his shoulders. The wee fella is eatin' an ice cream.

I look around me. And take strength from the great numbers. I hear someone say this is the biggest turnout yet. That they'd be mad to try to stop us. I hear someone else reply they *are* mad.

We're down from Creggan now. Near the bottom of William Street.

Me 'n' Andy turn with the march into Rossville Street. We snake along. Past the high flats. Near a barricade of rubble.

Suddenly! . . . behind us! . . . all hell breaks out!

The roar of armoured cars! The thud! thud! of rubber bullets! The smell of CS gas!

People scream . . . start to run . . . to stampede in all directions.

I look back . . . and see soldiers kneelin' in the open . . . takin' up firin' positions.

Then the thuds become sharper . . . become crack! crack! . . . and someone shouts the mad bastards are firin' live bullets!

Me 'n' Andy get split up. I look for shelter from this insane onslaught. People fall all about me. Some get up again and continue runnin'. Others lie still in pools of blood.

Crack! A bullet kicks up dust between me legs. And I realise that some anonymous assassin has *me* in his sights.

I scream, Maire. I pee me trousers. I cry out for mercy.

All around me the stench of cordite and gas . . . the smell of fear and death.

People runnin' . . . fallin' . . . crouchin' . . . prayin'.

I reach the sanctuary of the Rossville Flats doorway. And huddle there among the mass of tremblin' flesh. I close me eyes and think of you and Patrick, Maire. I cover me ears with me hands to blot out the sounds.

I don't want to die!

Oh, merciful Jesus, save me!

(*She pauses where she stands for a long moment, still staring out into the audience but in silence. Then, slowly, she turns and re-takes her seat. She drinks.*)

Later . . . someone would say that Bloody Sunday was the day innocence died in Derry. It was certainly the day *my* innocence died.

Over the next weeks and months . . . and years . . . a cloud hung over the city. It was like . . . like strangers had come into our house . . . had wrecked it . . . brutalised us . . . killed members of our family. And then just walked away scot-free.

But if they could only know the chaos and heartbreak they left behind.

# The Day Innocents Died

*Michael William Benson (2003)*

Innocently he rose from bed, just another day,
Breakfast first, TV next, then it's out to play.
Nine years old, he runs about oblivious to the world,
On the other side of the town a banner is unfurled.
He runs and plays, laughs and shouts, innocence in his mind,
Oblivious to what's going on or, later, to what he will find.
It's teatime now, he's had so much fun, tired he sits down.
TV on, what's on the news? There's murder in the town.
A priest waves a handkerchief, soldiers shoot their guns,
Thirteen dead on that day, next day another one.
Tired now he goes to bed, those pictures on his mind,
Thirty years of bloodshed, the next day he will find.

# A Long Auld Walk (extract)

*Laurence McClenaghan (2004)*

**Act Two**

*Betty Boland is waiting for her husband Kevin and son Billy to come home. Waiting with her is her daughter Denise and Mrs Doherty, an elderly neighbour. We join them in the Boland living room as they wait for news from the march. It has a small sparsely decorated bookshelf, a two-seater settee and a wooden armchair.*

*The occupants have heard that the army fired live ammunition in the Bogside, but they have no way of knowing if this has actually happened, where Billy and Kevin are or when, indeed if, they will make it home.*

*As the lights go up, Betty is pacing the floor, Denise is leaning against the scullery door at the rear of the stage and Mrs Doherty is sat on the edge of the two-seater. Her son, James, is perched on the sofa arm closest to his mother; their panic for their own loved ones has already passed.*

**Betty Boland:** What time is it now?

**Denise Boland:** Five to six, Ma. (*there is an awkward silence*) Ma, it'll be all right, he'll be home.

**Betty Boland:** If you tell me once more that it'll be all right, I won't be responsible, so help me this day.

**Denise:** But, Ma, Da is from England. (*the adults look at her, puzzled by the comment*) That means the Brits won't hurt them; he is going to be okay, sure.

**Betty Boland:** (*more exasperated than before*) Denise!

**Denise:** Sorry, Ma, I'm just trying (*her voice fades*) to help . . .

**Betty Boland:** Don't tell me not to worry, Denise. (*again she moves to behind the sofa*) Just leave it, go and get me a glass of water, will you. God, it's no wonder the whole town is going up the walls. Agh, Jesus, gone let my men come home. (*calling*) Denise, Denise. God, you're right, Mrs Doherty. (*and to herself*) Ah, Jesus, they've marched now, please, gone let them come home again. (*suddenly angry as she believes she is being ignored*) Denise! Denise! Are you not listening to me? Is that candle to Our Lady still lit?

**Denise:** (*part runs, part walks back into the room and frets past her mother*) Aye, Mammy, it is. Here's your water. (*Denise also hands her mother a small tub of tablets*) God, Mammy, you're shaking.

**Betty Boland:** Don't worry. (*taking a tablet from the bottle and washing it down*) This'll sort me out; I'll be grand. Denise, gone out to the kitchen and see if you can hear anything.

**Denise:** Ma, there'll be nothing on the set . . .

**Betty Boland:** (*loses her temper and begins shouting at her daughter*) Of course there will be! Why do you have to make this even harder? Don't you disobey me; there are people dead down there – of course they have to tell us what happened.

**Mrs Doherty:** Don't you worry yourself, Betty. Now, come on, the girl is just worried, too. (*to Denise*) Go you out to the wireless and have a wee listen, will you, just for your mammy, sure. Thanks, pet.
(*Denise only goes to the other side of the door; she is clearly already upset and her mother has, albeit inadvertently, made it worse*)

**Mrs Doherty:** (*impressed*) You handled that well; (*before teasing*) there might be hope for yours yet.

**Betty Boland:** Might there? Jesus, I nearly had her in tears when she was already past crying. She's worried about her brother and father the same way I am. I just should have known better . . . (*long pause, then quietly*) She is too young . . .

**Mrs Doherty:** Sure we're all too young for this, love . . . I don't seem to remember too much different. We hear something bad happens, then we wait to find out what happened, who is hurt and who isn't. Days like these are too much.

**Betty Boland:** At least we have each other to wait with, though . . .

**Mrs Doherty:** At least we have each other, she says. (*laughing*) Us girls have to stick together, is that it?

**Betty Boland:** Us girls have to stick together! Sure she'll be burning her bra next.
(*at that, there is a big smash as the living-room window is forced in; the women jump up and scream in fright before Mrs Doherty pulls Betty to the ground*)

**Mrs Doherty:** Jesus, Mary and Saint Joseph, the Brits are coming! Get down, they're shooting, Betty. Get down, love!
(*Denise comes running to the living-room door and her mother jumps up and attempts to protect her daughter; Mrs Doherty attempts to hold her*)

**Denise:** Ma, Ma, what happened? Who's coming? Are the Brits here?

**Betty Boland:** (*in desperation*) Stay there! Get down, love, please. (*Denise just stares out the window*)

**Mrs Doherty:** Jesus, they shot in the window! God have mercy on us all, they're trying to kill us! Ya bastards, have ye no God?

**Denise:** Ma, it's not the Brits – look . . .
(*at that, the two older women rise, slowly yet simultaneously, from the floor, never taking their eyes from what used to be the window; young Billy's face appears on the other side of the broken shards; he is moving even more slowly than the ladies, obviously more terrified than he has ever been in his short life*)

**Billy:** (*through the window*) I'm sorry, I . . . I didn't mean to . . . I didn't mean to make Mrs Doherty curse, Ma . . .

**Betty Boland:** That's okay, love, come on in. Come in here, will you. Where have you been, Billy?

**Billy:** (*he is obviously even more confused by his mother's actions and starts backing away from the window*) Mammy, I didn't mean it, Mammy. It was the ball – I didn't even see the window; I'm really sorry.

**Betty Boland:** Billy, it's okay, just come inside and we can sort this out. Come on in, love.

**Billy:** (*having made his mind up to flee*) No, Mammy, please don't hit me, it still hurts from earlier.
(*at that, Billy turns on his heels to run away again, but his mother erupts with a roar that scares him more than any beating he will ever face*)

**Betty Boland:** Billy Anthony Fitzpatrick Boland, you get inside this house this instance! If I have to come after you, so help me, your life will just not be worth living!
(*as Billy half-wanders half-plods his way into the house, crying and fearful of just how much of a beating he'll get, he wanders just inside the door before he is rushed by three girls who add their own tears of joy to his terrified shakes*)

**Betty Boland:** Billy, where have you been, son? And, Jesus, where is your da?
(*Lights down*)

# The Thief in the Night

*Paul Campbell (2005)*

Burned twice as bright for half as long,
braved life's fight with a hope-bound might.
But being sound of mind and ripe of soul,
can't guarantee you'll see another night.
For morals only serve the honest man
for the thief in the night steals whence he can.
No mother's face does the thief place
on the deeds on which he feeds his heart's crooked pace.

Dispel any notion that logic here applies,
for evil binds its kind in eternal alibi.
Memories fail when justice hunts the trail
or finds truth defunct beyond humane scale.
But truth will out in the heart devout,
even if apathy muffles the sob-draped shout.
One man's reason is another's reasonable doubt
but if there's a maker to meet he'll divvy it out.

The stone is mightier than bullet or bomb.
It wears humanity's plea on a bloodied bent knee.
But mightier still are one's own hands
if the fight fought is worthy, man to man.
For reason can be reached, compromise sought,
if each man keeps to his own grown plot.
'Take what you need, give what you can,'
save for the greed inherent in man.

Burned twice as bright for half as long,
all I've known of you ever, a sister's story, my song.
To the Stardust you raced on double-dates,
finding hand-in-hand life's reluctant grace.

Brother and sister, friend and friend,
and so it shall be beyond time's end.
'He's your guardian, son,' her words so wise,
'so greet him with the dawn, bid him farewell with night.'

Past day's demise, some essence must rise
to the home of song and laughter and heart-born cries.
Warmth there is in the wind's soft kiss,
in the crisp lain snow, in summer's hazed bliss.
'So offer up pain,' my mammy always said,
'for it softly lays the bed of those we know as dead.
Don't let evil's burden take another in vain,
or the shame and the killing will steal the breath from life again.

'Nor turn the other cheek, or live a life too meek,
just help the souls departed find the justice they seek.
Expose the absurdity of man's war on man,
by refusing the bait that begs the bite.
Don't let them snide "told you we were right",
as they rape, murder and shame in the blind dark of night.
Face them in the day so all can see
the crude strangling of humanity's plea.'

# Futility Reigns

*Aaron Phelan (2005)*

Draw the blinds, dress in black,
Wreaths arriving, no going back.
Guns have stuttered, the people fall,
See the shadowed lit candles on chapel wall.
Let hastened prayers speed heroes all
With churchyard bells' summoning call.
A mother's pallor, all was said,
A silent mind and body laid.
No glory, laughter, nor national pride,
For shattered lives that graves do hide.
All tempers and hate the dust consume,
No pounding heart, flag or pride,
Nor fisted gesture, for all have died.
A soldier's call to pass the test,
On clay bed now to rest,
A weeping heart, an outward cry,
Lonely maiden such morning as this.
Rip up the sun, blacken the sky,
There are more enlisted sons to die.
An exhausted mother alone,
Why?

# Reluctant Role Model

*Julieann Campbell (2005)*

While we grew up, oblivious and young
You were out there doing what couldn't be done.
Triumphant over adversity: Enemy state
British Rule of Law and all they dictate.
Achieving more than any ordinary citizen should –
Indeed – more than anyone thought you could.

Living mere yards from you all these years
It's easy to forget you are more than just an aunt.
While we fought your elder ways, you fought
Intimidation every day. In our name.
Campaigning for those most near and dear –
Lost siblings, lost innocence, the injustices were clear.
Thirty years of searching for the truth has almost ended
I hope and pray. Or you'll fight another day.

And should the time come when the struggle goes on . . .
Should you falter and lose your will to stay strong,
I'll stand in your place, continue the race –
Until our day comes.

## Bloody Sunday

*Charlie McLaughlin (2005)*

A march for peace and equality for all,
We did not think then that any would fall.
Shot like dogs on those Bogside streets,
By the so-called British Army elite.
Fathers, sons, brothers and sisters fell,
Most died that day in Derry's Hell.

To all those Brits who took part that day,
Irish history will surely say,
Murdering thugs to the very last man,
As evil as their predecessors, the Black and Tans.

When we bow our heads before sleep at night,
Think of those people who walked for right.
For their loved ones they only wanted the best,
God grant them eternal rest.

# Heroes With Their Hands in the Air (extract)
*Fintan Brady and Eamonn McCann (2007)*

**Scene Seven**

**John Kelly:** I had an opportunity, during the Inquiry, to tell Saville what my feelings were, and to pass onto him the feelings of my mother. That was a great relief to me.

**Kevin McDaid:** But, in the end, the Inquiry didn't happen the way Tony Blair promised. He said it would be wide open, and it wasn't. You had the Home Office and the MoD taking the Inquiry to court to prevent this coming out, that coming out.

**John Kelly:** We have seen the guys who perpetrated the killings brought in front of us, and seen civilians, hundreds, literally, after all the years, having the opportunity for the first time to tell their story. That's so important to the families.

**Kevin McDaid:** But it didn't answer all the questions. Why were they killed? Were the soldiers told to do it? Or did they just know what they were expected to do? The ordinary soldier could turn round and say, Well, he told me, or he told me. How far does it go? All the way back to Heath? Somebody has to answer.

**Patrick Nash:** Edward Heath knew what was happening and I feel he should be prosecuted. After all, they still chase Nazi war criminals.

**Eileen Greene:** As for our family, when the Report is published, that's it. The Report is the last kick of the ball. At that, this family is finished.

**Patrick Nash:** I just think it's right that if you commit a crime you have to pay and there's a lot of people should be paying.

**Eileen Greene:** I don't believe any Para will do a day.

**Liam Wray:** I don't believe that the truth about Bloody Sunday is going to come out in my time. I think we are going to get a partial truth which will satisfy many and I suppose in some terms will realise eighty percent of my dream. The fact that the Crown recognise that murder was committed remains important.

**John Kelly:** If I can't prosecute it won't be closure. We might have to go to Europe in the end. This could go on for years. I would love to be able to walk away and surround myself with my own family or whatever else I'm going to do. But there will be no sense of finality until F is prosecuted. I want F – the rest, too – but F, the murderer of my brother. I want him punished for what he did to my family. That's where I'm coming from. Maybe I am bitter.

**Liam Wray:** There was more times than enough I wanted to say, I am out of here, fuck this for toy soldiers. I see myself a lot older, worn out, angry and with a sense of futility – that's the worst.

**Johnny Campbell:** (*taking a letter from his pocket*) From Lord Saville, twenty-fourth of October, two thousand and six, 'We are grateful for the patience that the interested parties have shown since the hearings were concluded. We consider it most unlikely that we will complete the Report before the end of next year . . . at the earliest.' If we get all the names cleared, and the guilt put where the guilt should lie, we should put it all behind us and move on.

**Jimmy Duddy:** Hopefully, something will come out of this, not just for us but for all the other families everywhere in the world that these things have happened to. The military everywhere must be made to know that they are going to be accountable.

**Eileen Greene:** I suppose in a way we were lucky. You can look now at other things happening, here or anywhere in the world, and say, yes, those people deserve an Inquiry. But you know they are not going to get one. Not one like this one anyway. I don't think they'll ever grant another Inquiry like this. To be honest, just now, waiting for the Report, I'm scared. I think we all are. We're just not admitting it.

**Jimmy Duddy:** I saw on TV the day American troops took over a school. The villagers didn't want them, so they had a protest. The Americans killed thirteen or fourteen, some of them children of five or six. They said there was a gun battle, but there wasn't one bullet mark on the school. My mind went automatic – they're fucking lying, they murdered those people. This was Fallujah.

**Regina McKinney:** The only thing I want out of it now is for the men who were shot to go down in history as innocent. I think that is the only truth that we need. The Bloody Sunday soldiers are going to have to stand before God. I believe there will be a final judgement. My father will be justified. You see, I kind of think that my daddy died clean. He was shot with his hands up. I am proud the way my father died, not that he was shot but that he had his hands in the air, that he had nothing in his hands, that he did not retaliate. To me he is a hero. Every one of them was in their own right. Heroes.

**Geraldine Doherty:** I think I changed through the Inquiry, the more I learned about my uncle Gerard. I do have a real sense of him now, of a jolly, happy-go-lucky fellow full of fun and having a laugh. I think about the fact that he should be here, should have been married and had children, my cousins. I see him the way he was in the photographs, a tall, skinny fellow with a mop of long hair. I imagine him happy-go-lucky because that's the way my mum describes him, and from the stories she tells, of him pouring her good perfume down the toilet because he thought it was air freshener. I keep him in my mind like that, my mum shouting, 'God, Gerry! I'll kill you!' And him laughing his head off. I'm happy I have done as much as I have been able to make sure the lies they told about him didn't last, to make sure he is remembered as he truthfully was.

# I Am Told

*Niall Kelly (2007)*

I am told
we have the same eyes,
Yet we have never met.
I am told we have the same face,
Yet we have never spoken.
And I would.
If he told.

I am told
he was happy that day.
With his friends.
A beautiful clear day.
But that was his last day.
And it would not have been.
If he were told.

# THE WRITERS

### Anonymous – *Untitled*
This two-stanza poem was among the flood of condolence messages sent to the Wray family after the death of Jim Wray. The identity of its author, W McG – Bogsider, cannot be verified after all these years. In much the same way as Peggy Gough's poem, this piece sees the significance of the men's deaths in doubled terms: first as part of the longer, larger fight for Irish freedom, and second, as part of a more specific context of Civil Rights protest. The poem's slightness has the feel of a piece placed in the In Memoriam section of a newspaper. Donated to the collection by the Wray family.

### Anonymous – *Bloody Sunday Revisited*
Discovered in the archives of the Museum of Free Derry, *Bloody Sunday Revisited* is one of two anonymous pieces in this collection with few clues to their origin. The poem appears to have been written around 1992, as the author makes mention of *two decades later*, and there is a sense in which its speaker (and perhaps its author) is involved in news-gathering: she or he is visiting households in the Bogside twenty years after the events of Bloody Sunday.

Taking its cue from Yeats' interrogation of the double-edged notion of sacrifice, the poem senses the persistence of profound trauma amongst the survivors and amongst those who were not yet born in 1972. Although by 1992 the Bloody Sunday Justice Campaign had begun to take on a more proactive role in calling for a reopening of Widgery's findings, there remained, as the poem articulates, a widespread sense of depression in Derry fostered by the civil conflict and by the lack of any acceptable resolution to the obscenity of Bloody Sunday.

### Michael William Benson – *The Day Innocents Died*
At the time of Bloody Sunday, Michael Benson was a nine-year-old boy living in Clooney Estate in the Waterside. He later composed this poem about the effect that Bloody Sunday – his first experience of murder – had on him as an impressionable young boy. Benson believes that the events of 30 January 1972 had a traumatic effect on him, creating a deep resentment of state forces and causing him to have nightmares for most of his adult life. Michael Benson continues to write poetry and song on a regular basis.

### Fintan Brady and Eamonn McCann – *Heroes With Their Hands in the Air* (extract)
*Heroes With Their Hands in the Air* was premiered at the Playhouse in Derry in January 2007; it was directed by Fintan Brady. The play is an adaptation and a condensation of the many contributions made by the families of the dead of Bloody Sunday and by survivors of the day to journalist and author Eamonn McCann, who reproduced them in his 2006 book, *The Bloody Sunday Inquiry: the Families Speak Out*.

This extract picks up the action at the very end of the play, when the major characters voice their hopes and fears about the outcomes of an inquiry they tirelessly worked for, but from which, and to varying degrees, they felt alienated.

### Julieann Campbell – *Pablo's Part*
A reporter on the *Derry Journal*, Julieann Campbell has often returned in her poetry to the legacy of Bloody Sunday. *Pablo's Part*, the first of her two contributions to this collection, refers to her younger brother Paul's portrayal of their uncle, Jackie Duddy, in the Channel 4 drama-documentary *Sunday*, a role about which both Paul and the wider family circle were understandably very sensitive. Playing the part of his uncle is an anxiety-fraught experience for the actor: he retains control

until filming has ended, but then, in a moment of intense and uncanny connection with the elements of twenty-nine years earlier – false blood on the collar – finally succumbs to the emotional pressures implicit both in his role of actor and in his status of relative. In its controlled attention to these pressures, *Pablo's Part* is an intimate poem, finely alert to the complexity of family affiliations, memories and obligations.

## Julieann Campbell – *Reluctant Role Model*

*Reluctant Role Model* was written in tribute to Kay Duddy, aunt and next-door neighbour of the collection's co-editor Julieann Campbell. Kay was an integral member of the Bloody Sunday Justice Campaign and has shown incredible strength and determination in the years since Bloody Sunday. She has relentlessly campaigned alongside other relatives in pursuit of the truth and eventually handed a petition to British Prime Minister Tony Blair, resulting in the establishment of a second inquiry.

*Reluctant Role Model* is part of that strand of poetry – well attested in this collection – in which Bloody Sunday has been handed down to later generations as part of a family's, and a community's, history. With a mixture of awe and belated recognition, and with a purposeful sense of solidarity with a figure who has, for decades, remained focused on the need for justice, the poem promises to continue Kay Duddy's work until, in a rejuvenation and a resituating of the Republican phrase, *our day comes.*

## Paul Campbell – *Uncle Jackie*

Musician and art teacher Paul Campbell has always identified with his uncle, Jackie Duddy, who died on Bloody Sunday. Besides the two having shared a passion for boxing, Paul also had the poignant honour of portraying his late uncle in Jimmy McGovern and Charles McDougall's Channel 4 drama *Sunday* in 2001. The song *Uncle Jackie* was composed in the months following the often difficult filming of the drama-documentary.

Campbell's narrative poem focuses on the family debate about participating in the march on 30 January 1972 and on the craic that was to be had by Jackie Duddy and his friend John Young. The poem concludes with Jackie's final gesture – a laugh as he sees himself overtaken by a youthful Father Daly – and with the abrupt announcement of his death.

### Paul Campbell – *The Thief in the Night*

The second contribution from Paul Campbell gives a sombre and complexly constructed meditation on the nature of loss, interweaved with glimpses of the life of his uncle, Jackie Duddy. An embellished conversation undertaken with the poet's mother, the piece moves from a sense of near despair to an optimistic but hard-headed ethical response to state violence. As such, it is something of a visionary poem.

### Dan Baron Cohen/Derry Frontline – *Obráid Domhnach Na Fola/Operation Bloody Sunday*

Dan Baron Cohen co-founded and worked with Frontline: Culture and Education in Manchester (1986–89) and Derry (1988–94). Its cultural self-determination methods were inspired by the writings of, among others, Paulo Freire, Edward Bond and Irish Republican political prisoners. As a community-based organisation, Derry Frontline used theatre, sculpture, murals, banners, storytelling, poetry and intercultural workshops to enable young unemployed participants and their communities (mainly from the Bogside and Creggan) to 'establish a critical distance on their most sensitive and controversial experience' and 'to question and understand their most deeply-rooted cultural traditions.' Their plays, *Inside Out*, *Time Will Tell* and *Threshold*, and their many murals on the back of Free Derry Corner, aimed to contribute to a culture of self-determination. Derry Frontline's plays were published by Guildhall Press in 2001 in the collection *Theatre of Self-Determination*. This is the only piece in the collection to have been translated into the Irish language.

## Da Willie Folk – *Rossville Street Sunday*

A popular Derry-based group in the early 1970s, Da Willie Folk consisted of Neil (Da Willie) Doherty, Gerry McGowan, Sean McGowan, Declan O'Donnell and John McCool. Coincidentally, Da Willie Folk were actually performing in the Derry City Social Club on Bishop Street the very morning of Bloody Sunday, when the club was raided by the Paras.

The song's opening – in which the names of the dead are recited – ties the piece very closely to the moments at which the dead were named on the evening of 30 January 1972 in radio and television reports, in newspaper print over the following days and in the prayers for the dead in the requiem Mass. It is a striking feature that occurs time and again in the pieces collected in this book, and its chief function is to remind the listener or reader that this was a tragedy that happened not in the abstract but to individuals caught up in the terrible events of that day.

## Seamus Deane – *After Derry, 30 January 1972*

Best known perhaps for his 1996 novel *Reading in the Dark*, Seamus Deane is one of Ireland's foremost literary critics. He is the Donald and Marilyn Keough Professor of Irish Studies at the University of Notre Dame, Indiana, and a director of the Field Day Company. On 30 January 1997, Deane chaired the "Secrets and Lies: 25 Years On" symposium during that year's Bloody Sunday commemorative events.

Born in the Bogside, Deane's work returns frequently to the history and terrain of his native town. This poem articulates with a steely precision the sense of trauma in the days following the killings. It also predicts what in fact turned out to be one of the most notable after-effects of Bloody Sunday:

the radicalisation of thousands of young people and their turn towards the Provisional IRA.

### Mary J Devlin – *McGuigan*

Mary Josephine Devlin was born in 1935 in Fahan, County Donegal, and spent twenty years as organist in the Church of St Aengus in nearby Burt. Written on 2 February 1972, this particular poem responds to one of the most horrific images of Bloody Sunday: Bernard McGuigan lying dead by the telephone box by the Rossville Flats. McGuigan was shot in the head as he ventured out to assist Patrick Doherty, himself fatally wounded by the Paratrooper now identified as Soldier F. This is the first time *McGuigan* has been published. Now living in Burt, County Donegal, Devlin continues to write the occasional verse in her retirement.

### Mary J Devlin – *Derry*

This poem, written by Mary Josephine Devlin as she sat in Duddy's café on the Strand Road, Derry, in February 1974, articulates perfectly the sense of depression and hopelessness that descended on Derry following the initial optimism of the Civil Rights movement. Although the poem commemorates the waste of so many lives in the city during the early days of the Troubles, it focuses specifically, as its author informed the editors, on the dead of Bloody Sunday.

### Gerry Dorrity – *One Sunday*

Originally from Gobnascale in the Waterside area of the city, Gerry Dorrity married a woman from the Bogside and for the past twenty years has accompanied his father-in-law to Bloody Sunday commemoration marches. While *One Sunday* speaks of *my Daddy and his Dad*, the imaginary narrative actually refers to his own son, who also attends marches with his father and grandfather, and their inherited reasoning with regard to the importance of the annual marches.

'This conversation never actually took place, but it could have,' Dorrity says. More poignant still is the fact that the author's son performed this very piece at the Derry Féis several years ago.

Gerry Dorrity has been involved with drama groups for over twenty years, touring Ireland with both the '71 Players and Field Day theatre companies. Having recently developed an interest in writing, he has penned a number of short stories and poems and is currently working on a novel and play.

## Jackie Duddy – *Looking Back to the Future*

Nephew and namesake of his uncle who was killed on Bloody Sunday, Jackie Duddy received a certificate for this poem after entering it, aged twelve, in a secondary-school competition. Jackie says he loved English class when he was a pupil at St Brigid's High School and that he is particularly proud of this Bloody Sunday poem, as it is a subject 'close to the heart.' In 2002, Jackie was cast as the Counsel in Dave Duggan's play *Scenes From an Inquiry*, which ran at the Playhouse in Derry.

In this poem, the ghost of the late Jackie Duddy returns from the undead state in which all ghosts exist to comment on how time has treated his native city. The poem's prosaic details are heightened and made poignant by the absolute sense of loss voiced by Duddy's ghost. Unlike many literary spectres, the ghost of Jackie Duddy does not issue a reprimand for a failure of justice but acts as a rather more straightforward reminder of the abruptness of a life lost at such a young age. It should be noted how, unlike many literary ghosts, Jackie's ghost is entirely devoid of self-pity.

## Jackie Duddy – *The Grief of Derry*

*The Grief of Derry* is the second poem written by Jackie Duddy, nephew of Bloody Sunday victim Jackie Duddy, while a fifteen-year-old pupil at St Brigid's High School.

Duddy's line *cold unknown surroundings* links this poem to his first contribution to the collection (in which the ghost of his uncle returns to Derry). But unlike his earlier piece, there is little sense of optimism here in a poem that gathers together all the lies and silences of Bloody Sunday into its final, single and simple question: why?

### Eugene Duffy – *Bloody Sunday, 30 January 1972*
Originally from Little Diamond on the edge of Derry's Bogside, Eugene Duffy felt compelled to write *Bloody Sunday, 30 January 1972* in the weeks after Bloody Sunday as he tried to come to terms with the events of the day. Having been on the march and having witnessed first-hand the panic in the streets, Eugene captures in this poem how rapidly the mood changed as the Paratroopers swarmed into Rossville Street. An Irish Amateur Boxing Association (IABA) and international referee, Eugene has spent a lifetime in boxing and is now the Honorary Registrar of the Ulster Provincial Council of the IABA. He donated this poem to the archives of the Bloody Sunday Trust many years ago.

### Dave Duggan – *Scenes From an Inquiry* (extract)
Dramatist and novelist Dave Duggan, originally from Waterford, wrote *Scenes From an Inquiry* for Sole Purpose Productions to mark the thirtieth anniversary of Bloody Sunday in 2002. He felt the language of the legal process of the Saville Inquiry was inadequate to the emotional and mythic dimensions of the events of Bloody Sunday and that theatre could offer the heightened language necessary. Witness was played by Sarah Wray, niece of the late Jim Wray, and Counsel was played by Jackie Duddy, nephew of the late Jackie Duddy. Caoimhe Farren played the Judge. Duggan subsequently wrote a radio version, which RTÉ Radio Drama broadcast in 2003.

### John Dunne – *Tribute to Lord Fenner-Brockway*

Retired schoolteacher John Dunne uses Seamus Heaney's *For the Commander of the Eliza* as a model – and war poet Wilfred Owen as the inspiration – for *Tribute to Lord Fenner-Brockway*. This poem also echoes many of the concerns and the linguistic traits of Thomas Kinsella's *Butcher's Dozen*.

Born in Derry, John has been greatly influenced by the events of 30 January 1972 and has written several detailed features and articles on both Bloody Sunday and the Battle of the Bogside for the *Derry Journal*. It is in the nature of poets to opt for the unobvious subject; and nowhere is this truer than in John Dunne's tribute to Lord Fenner-Brockway, a British Labour Party lord who was due to give a speech at the planned rally in Guildhall Square. Bloody Sunday begins for Dunne at the moment in which Fenner-Brockway's speech was cancelled by the Paras' incursion into the Bogside. At that moment, a decisive shift – from words to war – occurs. It is no accident that a poem beginning with such humane concern for the safety for an elderly English lord should conclude with an injunction to another English lord, Mark Saville, to this time assert the truth.

### Brian Foster – *Maire – A Woman of Derry* (extract)

Brian Foster is a professional playwright with several productions to his name. *Maire – A Woman of Derry* has played throughout Ireland and the United States. When it played at Derry's Playhouse Theatre and the Millennium Forum Theatre, it broke box-office records in both venues.

Maire is a middle-aged street alcoholic, and in her monologue it becomes clear how large a role Bloody Sunday played in her downfall. In this extract, Maire recounts her ex-husband Tommy's terrified story of the events of the day from an eyewitness point of view. Much of the action and many of the characters in the play are amalgamations of real people and real events, and much of Tommy's account is drawn from Brian

Foster's own experiences of being at the march on 30 January 1972. His best friend, Willie Nash, died on that day.

## Brian Friel – *The Freedom of the City* (extract)

Playwright Brian Friel was born in 1929 in Omagh, County Tyrone. Moving to Derry at the age of ten, he was educated at St Columb's College. He is the author of internationally acclaimed plays such as *Philadelphia Here I Come!* (1964), *Translations* (1980), and *Dancing at Lughnasa* (1990).

Friel's play *The Freedom of the City* (1973) concerns the shooting dead by the British Army of three unarmed Civil Rights protestors on a Saturday in February in 1970. The action takes place in and around the Guildhall and centres on the differing, and sometimes conflicting, aspirations of Michael, Skinner and Lily, who find themselves holed up in the mayor's parlour after the protest march and rally had been attacked by British soldiers. Although ostensibly concerned with a fictitious event, Friel's play is full of uncanny echoes of the events of 30 January 1972. In this extract, Michael, Lily and Skinner face the audience to describe their deaths. It is an unforgettable and profoundly moving moment of theatre.

## Hugh Gallagher – *Bloody Sunday*

*Bloody Sunday*, the first of two pieces by Hugh Gallagher, was written around the tenth anniversary of the event. The first poem in the collection touches upon the hope and naivety of all those, including Hugh himself, who took part in the original Civil Rights march on 30 January 1972.

'We really believed that by marching that day, we could actually achieve something and get rights from the British Government,' Hugh said. He is the author of many short stories, a book entitled *The Spectator and Other Derry Stories*, published by Yes! Publications, and is a regular contributor to local newspapers, the *Derry Journal* and the *Sentinel* among others.

### Hugh Gallagher – *Bloody Sunday*
Also entitled *Bloody Sunday*, Hugh Gallagher's second piece details the despondency felt by many people on the day of the funerals. Using brutally honest, emotive language, Hugh recalls the anger and disbelief evoked when the majority of seats for the funerals in St Mary's Chapel were reserved for Free State dignitaries, forcing countless Derry people to gather outside in the wind and rain to pay their last respects.

### Peggy Gough – *Bloody Sunday*
This poem, signed by Peggy Gough, seems to have been written in the immediate aftermath of Bloody Sunday and then given to the Wray family as a condolence for the death of Jim Wray.

Among the details of the march itself and the incursion of the Paras into the Bogside are interesting moments in which the apparent straightforwardness of the narrative is complicated. For example, Gough sees the actions of the Paras on Bloody Sunday as a betrayal of prouder moments in the regiment's history, such as its gallantry at the battle of Arnhem in 1944. Indeed, an awareness of history that is never far from many of these poems is present, too, in Peggy Gough's piece, as when she invokes the memory and the spirit of two heroes of Irish resistance – Pearse and Lafferty – to British occupation.

### Seamus Heaney – *The Road to Derry*
Nobel Laureate Seamus Heaney grew up in County Derry and was educated at St Columb's College. *The Road to Derry* has never been included in any collection and lay unread for many years before it was first published when Heaney sent it to the *Derry Journal* for the Bloody Sunday twenty-fifth commemoration edition. In a letter to the newspaper, Heaney revealed that Luke Kelly of the Dubliners had asked him to write a song in the wake of the massacre: 'I did four

stanzas . . . and sent them to him, with the suggestion that they might be put to the air of *The Boys of Mullaghbawn*, but nothing ever came of it . . . Anyway, I think it is in order to reprint this abbreviated version now, twenty-five years after the drive from Belfast to Derry on the day of the funerals.'

### Seamus Heaney – *Casualty*

By the time his 1979 volume *Field Work* was published, Seamus Heaney was establishing himself alongside Michael Longley as among the foremost elegists of victims of the Northern Irish conflict.

*Casualty* is an outstanding example of Heaney's turn toward the elegiac mood and poetic function. Nowhere is Heaney's ability to accommodate multiple perspectives as evident as here, in a poem that is a memorial to the dead of Bloody Sunday, and also to a friend who died in an explosion in the days following the killings.

Louis O'Neill died on the day of the funerals (Wednesday, 2 February 1972) in a Provisional IRA bomb attack on the Imperial Bar in Stewartstown, County Tyrone. A regular drinker in the bar, O'Neill paid the price for breaking the IRA-announced curfew: *How culpable was he / That last night when he broke / Our tribe's complicity?* Heaney asks. In this beautifully handled and hugely humane poem, Heaney acknowledges the terrible and complicated ramifications of the Paratroopers' actions a few days earlier in Derry.

### Niall Kelly – *I Am Told*

Derry musician Niall Kelly composed this short piece *I Am Told* as a subtle musical tribute to his uncle, Michael Kelly, who was killed on Bloody Sunday. Niall says that his late uncle has been a 'constant memory' in his life, despite the two never having met.

The piece has added poignancy, considering Niall shares not only a birthday and close resemblance with Michael, but he was also chosen to play the role of his seventeen-year-old uncle in Jimmy McGovern's 2001 drama-documentary *Sunday*. Niall Kelly is a full-time musician and lives in England.

It is fitting that this collection closes with a quiet meditation – from a songwriter who was not yet born on 30 January 1972 – on the ties that bind generations of the same family. To be sure, this poem has its ambiguity, but what is communicated above all is a conjoined sense of loss, subtly articulated pride, and connection across time with Michael Kelly, shot dead as he stood on the low rubble barricade on Rossville Street. It is a stunning, and at the same time understated, poem.

## Berni Kerr – *William Street, Derry, January 2002 (After Yeats et al)*

Berni Kerr was born in Dungannon, County Tyrone, and has vivid memories of sitting in front of the television, surrounded by family and neighbours, as news of the killings in Derry first broke. Kerr says her poem was created around the thirtieth anniversary when, whilst standing in the late-night taxi queue in William Street's "Aggro Corner", she was struck by the thought of the first fatal victim, Jackie Duddy, being shot and carried to safety nearby. The poem is influenced by other Irish poets writing of the Irish struggle, in particular WB Yeats' *Easter 1916*.

Berni Kerr has also written the plays *Do You Take Sugar?* and *Moan Quietly If At All* for the Playhouse in Derry. Her poem *The Perfect Mother* was shortlisted for the Hennessy award for emerging Irish writers in 2001.

## Thomas Kinsella – *Butcher's Dozen: A Lesson for the Octave of Widgery*

Born in Dublin in 1928, Thomas Kinsella has published numerous poetry collections throughout his career and now lives in Philadelphia. One of the great political poems produced in Ireland in the twentieth century, Kinsella's ballad *Butcher's Dozen* was written and printed within seven days of the publication of Lord Widgery's Report in April 1972. Kinsella speaks with the ghosts of the Bloody Sunday dead in a poem that is, by turns, bitter, analytical, despairing and finally (perhaps) hopeful.

The poem was published by Kinsella's newly founded Peppercanister Press as a pamphlet (costing ten pence) and bore on its front cover the design of the badge issued at the 6 February 1972 Civil Rights march and rally at Newry. The badge was in the shape of a black coffin with the number thirteen superimposed upon it.

### Emmylou Large – *Let the Stones Speak*
Emmylou Large's poem is resolutely in the tradition of poetry inaugurated by William Blake and carried forward by poets such as Emily Dickinson, Zbigniew Herbert, Ted Hughes and Derek Mahon. This is the tradition in which, in Mahon's resonant phrase, 'the mute phenomena' are allowed consciousness and are given poetic voice.

Large's poem is a superb act of imagination in which a single piece of stone dislodged from Free Derry Corner observes the deteriorating situation in Rossville Street. The stone offers a clear-sighted eyewitness report of the actions of the Paras before it is plucked from the street and thrown as a meagre response to the bullets fired from the soldiers' SLRs.

### Paul Laughlin – *Remembering Bloody Sunday*
Paul Laughlin was fifteen at the time of Bloody Sunday. Although not present on the march, he explains the significance of the killings to the community of which he was a part: 'The stark reality of state murder in the town where I lived and on the streets which I travelled every day to school obviously had an enormous impact and was a

formative influence in shaping my political consciousness. Nor could I fail to see that the manner in which the victims of state violence had been treated was hugely significant in defining the attitudes of a generation towards the British state in Ireland.' In 1995, Paul was invited to read *Remembering Bloody Sunday* at the Poets' Panel of the Cuirt International Literary Festival in Galway.

### John Lennon and Yoko Ono – *Sunday Bloody Sunday*

*Sunday Bloody Sunday* featured on Lennon and Ono's SOMETIME IN NEW YORK CITY, the album that marked a decisive shift in the couple's engagement with radical politics. Co-produced by Phil Spector and recorded between January and March 1972, SOMETIME IN NEW YORK CITY is a collection of songs deeply concerned with some of the most blatant social injustices in the United States and elsewhere. Two songs – *The Luck of the Irish* and *Sunday Bloody Sunday* – widen the album's concerns beyond the US. In the first, the blistering anti-colonialism of the lyric belies the romantic lyricism of the musical arrangement, whilst the second, *Sunday Bloody Sunday*, stands as one of the finest republican ballads of recent times.

### Eoghan MacCormaic – *Marchers*

Born in Derry in 1955, Eoghan MacCormaic spent fifteen years in the H Blocks from 1976 to 1991 during which time he wrote many poems and two novels. He has a degree in Celtic Studies from the National University of Ireland, Galway. *Marchers* was first published in *The Best of the West*, a selection of the top entries in the 1989 Creative Writing Competition of the West Belfast Festival. This publication was brought to the editors' attention by Ross Moore of the Northern Ireland Political Collection at the Linen Hall Library, Belfast. Married with four children and currently living in Galway, Eoghan has had a number of books in Irish published, and also articles and poetry in various anthologies.

MacCormaic's poem celebrates the steadfastness of those who for so many years paced the route of the original march in commemoration of the fallen of Bloody Sunday. It is, in essence, an optative poem that retains the spirit, the dynamism, and the political consciousness of the Civil Rights march and proposed rally at Guildhall Square on 30 January 1972.

### Thomas McCarthy – *Counting the Dead on the Radio*

Born and raised in Waterford, Thomas McCarthy is a poet, novelist and critic who now lives in Cork. He has published several collections of poetry with Anvil Press, including *The Non-Aligned Storyteller* (1984) from which this poem is selected.

With the exception, perhaps, of Paul Durcan, no other poet has analysed so carefully and unremittingly the politics of the Southern state; indeed, the poet Eavan Boland has said that McCarthy is the first poet born in the Republic to write about it so critically. Much of McCarthy's work considers the effects of the intrusion of politics into the family and here, in *Counting the Dead on the Radio*, the events in Derry produce effects that are by turns subtle and devastating. Much of the poem's eerie power relies on how the reader interprets its final sentence.

### John F McCartney – *Injustice*

Now retired, John F McCartney devoted many years to teaching in St Columb's College, Thornhill College, and the North West Institute of Further and Higher Education. He has always been keen on writing and has composed a book of short stories called *Tales of the River Faughan*, a book on the history of Pennyburn, and a locally inspired novel called

*Fufteen.* John has had poetry published in *Waterside Voices*, *Ireland's Eye* and dozens of anthologies.

Published originally in his 1998 anthology *Poetry of Passing Thoughts*, *Injustice* is a vivid eyewitness rendering of the events of Bloody Sunday. Its shocking imagery is suddenly undercut in the final stanza with its author's confident assertion of both national liberation and equal rights for all.

### Laurence McClenaghan – *A Long Auld Walk* (extract)

*A Long Auld Walk*, written by Laurence McClenaghan, was first staged at Derry's Playhouse Theatre as part of the Bloody Sunday commemoration programme in 2004. The play examines the impact of Bloody Sunday on one family whose father happens to be English. As news of the day's tragic events filters back to homes throughout the city, an anxious Boland family await their loved ones' return from the tragic march.

Laurence McClenaghan was born and raised in Derry and is now a reporter for the *Derry Journal*. He has written and staged several other plays.

### Paddy McCourt – *They Were Better Than Most*

Paddy McCourt was twenty-five when he wrote *They Were Better Than Most* and he believes the piece captures a certain innocence of language and a naive idea of social justice, now abandoned with adulthood. Paddy says he learned a great deal about Bloody Sunday from his parents, from close friends of the family, particularly Kay Duddy (sister of Jackie Duddy), and from social commentators such as Eamonn McCann.

Each sentence in the poem highlights different aspects of Bloody Sunday, which its author had experienced or never experienced. For example, the opening sentences tell the reader that the author wasn't born at the time of Bloody Sunday but that he still commemorated it, demonstrating the power of memory within the Nationalist community. According to Paddy McCourt, the poem's title refers to 'something I always picked up from the victims' relatives, particularly Kay Duddy, who told me Jackie was a great boxer – in fact, he was better than most boxers his age.'

### Perry McDaid – *A Disarming Suggestion*
Creggan poet and writer Perry McDaid had always regarded writing as a form of therapy. His contributions to this book add to the many poems and twenty-three short stories he has had published to date. In 1972, Perry was in his first year at college and the events of Bloody Sunday had a profound effect on him: 'The days following were a revelation to me, first-hand reports and chilling embellishments filling my ears; my great aunt still traumatised from what she had seen and heard happening outside her own door.'

His first poem in this collection, *A Disarming Suggestion*, takes a decidedly jaundiced view of the decommissioning negotiations occurring around the turn of the millennium. Part of its sceptical vision relates back to the shocking scenes of people cowering like animals from the Paras' bullets on Bloody Sunday. More so perhaps than any other contribution, McDaid's poem is situated in the abject horror of the panicking crowd, a horror that has tangibly shaped the poet's political consciousness in the years that followed.

### Perry McDaid – *Muted Martyrs*
This second thought-provoking piece by Creggan poet and writer Perry McDaid, *Muted Martyrs*, uses as its focus the obelisk-shaped memorial to Bloody Sunday that stands on Rossville Street. As daily events carry on around it, the memorial maintains a silent and often unregarded vigil. McDaid senses the tremendously dignified nature of this particular memorial that comes to take on an almost natural

sense of permanence. *Muted Martyrs* was previously published in *Reach Magazine* (November 2001).

**Robert McDaid and Patrick O'Doherty** – ***No Longer Cry***
Robert McDaid and Patrick O'Doherty co-wrote *No Longer Cry* in 2001, inspired by their experiences of playing extras in Paul Greengrass' feature film *Bloody Sunday*. They also submitted the song to the film's producers for consideration for the soundtrack. The experience brought back painful memories for Patrick in particular, as his sister's boyfriend, Michael Kelly, had been among those killed on Bloody Sunday. The pair found that composing the song helped them express their feelings about the horror and injustice of Bloody Sunday.

This is the only piece in the collection that makes the crucial link between the aims of the Northern Ireland Civil Rights movement and those of the American Civil Rights campaigns, led by Dr Martin Luther King. Both Robert and Patrick have spent years as unpaid volunteers running the Creggan Guitar Club.

**Joe McGrory** – *Anniversary*
Retired school teacher Joe McGrory was on the Civil Rights march with friends when, just a few metres from where they stood in the Rossville Flats car park, they witnessed the shooting of Bloody Sunday's first fatal victim, Jackie Duddy. Joe McGrory later gave evidence of this event to the Saville Inquiry.

As the first anniversary of Bloody Sunday passed, he says he felt compelled to mark the occasion with the poem *Anniversary*, a piece that he always kept and has uncovered only now. Joe McGrory has been published on many occasions during his career as a teacher of Speech and Drama at St Columb's College.

Joe McGrory's poem looks back at the events of Bloody Sunday a year earlier. The well-attested sense of despondency that fell upon Derry following the killings and Widgery's whitewash of those killings is leavened by the poem's closing rallying call, in which the cause of Brian Boru is revivified as the only possible response to what happened that day in Derry.

### Frank McGuinness – *Carthaginians* (extract)

Playwright Frank McGuinness wrote *Carthaginians* in 1988 as a direct response to events in Derry that, as he said in an introduction to the play, '. . . ripped Ireland apart . . . My adolescence ended that day.' A play full of humour and pain, *Carthaginians* is, as McGuinness says, an 'elegy to the dead and the living of Derry, the living who kept going, in Dido's words, ". . . surviving. Carthage has not been destroyed."'

The action of the play takes place in the City Cemetery over a week of sweltering weather in August 1984. Three women spend their time there waiting on a vision and attended by a group of men all bearing, to varying extents, the scars of their experiences of the Troubles.

Towards its close, *Carthaginians* shifts decisively from dramatic theatre to poetry. At first the shift seems casual enough, but within seconds of Paul and Seph discussing their admiration of poetry, the names of the Bloody Sunday dead are recited by Paul. In the first published version of the play, the names are punctuated by characters questioning the effects of Bloody Sunday upon their own lives, but in McGuinness' preferred version (the version reproduced here), the names of the dead retain an integrity by being recited in exactly the same fashion as every commemorative vigil at the memorial at Joseph Place.

### Charlie McLaughlin – *Bloody Sunday*

Originally from Derry's Bogside, Charlie McLaughlin spent years coming to terms with the harrowing events of Bloody Sunday and often found solace in art as a means of expression.

He held his first solo exhibition of oil paintings, entitled *Murder on a Sunday*, in Derry's Gasyard Centre in spring 2005. This poem was composed the same year and moves dramatically and emphatically from anger to hope of historical vindication, to subdued pathos and, finally, to prayer.

### Declan McLaughlin – *Running Uphill*

Derry singer-songwriter Declan McLaughlin wrote *Running Uphill* as a protest song whilst a member of the band The Screaming Bin Lids. The song also featured on a special commemorative CD produced by the Bloody Sunday Trust in 2000 entitled TIME FOR TRUTH. Its inclusion on a CD with this title is remarkably apt for a song that is marked by a powerful commitment to justice and truth.

Much of its narrative concerns the need, and indeed the duty, to commemorate the dead and to call for the truth of the circumstances of their deaths to be fully recognised by participating in the annual march: a form of protest particularly well-suited to the circumstances of Bloody Sunday. To march along the route of the original parade is to connect across time with the participants of the original protest, not simply in a re-enactment but in an act of solidarity. McLaughlin's song asserts both the monotony and the quiet heroism of this simple act of remembrance.

### Michael McLaughlin – *Bloody Sunday*

Michael McLaughlin, from Fountain Hill in the Waterside, was a father of eight and a joiner by trade in Derry's Tillie and Henderson shirt factory. Michael was admitted to hospital only days after Bloody Sunday and died in August of that year. His son, Patsy, revealed that although his father was not a well-educated man, he had an exceptional gift for verse and dictated his poem, *Bloody Sunday*, to his children from his hospital bed.

Michael McLaughlin's poem is one of several in this collection to draw parallels between the events in Derry and those in Dublin on 21 November 1920 in which more than thirty people lost their lives, including the assassination of fourteen British agents of the Cairo Gang and the retaliation of the British Army in Croke Park in which fifteen innocent civilians were shot dead. The poem was donated to the collection by the McLaughlin family.

### JP McMenamin – *The Story of Bloody Sunday in Verse* (extract)

Originally from County Tyrone, retired mill worker John Paul McMenamin found himself compelled to write the self-published *The Story of Bloody Sunday in Verse* in 2001. Besides Bloody Sunday receiving a great deal of media coverage that year, his nephew Ciaran McMenamin was cast in the lead role of Leo Young in Jimmy McGovern's drama-documentary *Sunday*.

This extract echoes Hugh Gallagher's sentiments concerning the outrageous decision to allocate so many seats at the requiem Mass in St Mary's Chapel for dignitaries, while relatives, friends, fellow marchers, and other mourners were left to stand outside in the biting rain.

### Sharon Meenan and Killian Mullan – *I Wasn't Even Born*

One of the most notable elements of the twenty-fifth anniversary commemorative events was this poem written by two young people from Derry. Sharon Meenan and Killian Mullan's *I Wasn't Even Born* was featured both in the *Derry Journal* supplement and in the Pat Finucane Centre's publicity leaflet for the weekend's programme. Deployed alongside the banners, the poem provided one of the most dramatic moments of all Bloody Sunday commemorations.

As the dead men were named in the poem, the Bogside Artists' banners of shimmering images of their faces were raised on the hill overlooking Free Derry Corner.

### Christy Moore – *Minds Locked Shut*

Legendary Irish folk musician Christy Moore composed this song in 1996, including it in his album GRAFFITI TONGUE later the same year. He also continues to perform the song regularly when on tour. In his 2000 autobiography, *One Voice – My Life in Song*, Christy Moore said of Bloody Sunday, 'I went over to England to tour when the Widgery Report came out and I was shocked by the number of English people who believed that the fourteen shot dead on Bloody Sunday were IRA men.'

The musician's disbelief and abhorrence of the events of 30 January 1972 is evident in the lyrics, where the emphasis is on the unexpected violence *on a lovely bright winter's afternoon.*

### L Morris – *Sunday Stones*

*Sunday Stones* was first performed in 1986 by Derry-based band NFF. More recently, the lyrics came to light when a special commemorative copy of them was distributed to hundreds of people as a token of appreciation for all who took part in the re-enactment of the original Bloody Sunday march during the filming of Jimmy McGovern and Charles McDougall's *Sunday*.

There is in this song a condensed and understated history of both the development and the death, following Bloody Sunday, of the Civil Rights movement as a potent force. Morris' steadfast emphasis on the initial concerns of the many and diverse groups that made up the Civil Rights movement in Northern Ireland – *houses, jobs and votes* – is shattered as the speech of the marchers is replaced by the stones of the rioters, and as those stones are themselves replaced by the bullets of the army. The song is also a poignant parable of the journey from innocence to experience; a journey that in the case of many young people in Derry was hastened to an exponential degree by the events of Bloody Sunday.

## Paul Muldoon – *The Year of the Sloes, For Ishi*

Paul Muldoon was born in 1951 in County Armagh and was educated at Queen's University, Belfast. In 1987, he moved to New Jersey, where he has lived and worked ever since. He is the Howard GB Clark '21 University Professor in the Humanities, and Professor of Creative Writing in the Centre for the Creative and Performing Arts at Princeton University. Paul Muldoon has published many collections of poetry and won the 2003 Pulitzer Prize for his collection *Moy Sand and Gravel* (2002).

Written 'as a direct response to Bloody Sunday', Muldoon's *The Year of the Sloes, For Ishi* forges subtle but suggestive parallels between the fate of the Derry Civil Rights protestors and that of the last remaining members of a native North American community slaughtered by US cavalry. At the time of writing the poem, Muldoon was reading Dee Brown's *Bury My Heart at Wounded Knee: An Indian History of the American West*.

## Paul Muldoon – *Herm*

While explicit reference to Bloody Sunday may only be fleeting in this beautiful lyric poem, the very swiftness by which one of the icons of that day (Father Daly's white handkerchief) is introduced produces a sense of shocked recognition. Like many of Muldoon's poems, *Herm* does not reveal its meanings in any immediate or obvious sense; yet the tone of anguish is undeniable. In this ambiguous and, frankly, difficult poem, the sudden appearance of Father Daly is startling because he is introduced as a substantial character, as the priest who *reels among those mown down in Derry*. *Herm* appeared in Muldoon's Pulitzer Prize-winning collection *Moy Sand and Gravel* (2002).

## Joe Mulheron – *Bloody Sunday*

Derry musician Joe Mulheron wrote this song some months after Bloody Sunday, using the air of an aptly named Woody Guthrie song, *1913 Massacre*. The song was recorded by The Men of No Property, the folk band of which he was a member. It was released on their own Resistance Records label. The song, performed in *seannós* style by folk singer Eileen Webster, later featured on a special commemorative CD produced by the Bloody Sunday Trust in 2000 entitled TIME FOR TRUTH.

Mulheron's song has no doubts about the political motivations of the army's actions that day and lays the blame squarely at the door of British Prime Minister Edward Heath. While this view took on considerable currency in the years following Bloody Sunday, it is a bitter irony that Mulheron's poem voices a strong communal knowledge years before concrete evidence of the deliberate policy of shoot-to-kill came to light. It is in this context of state involvement in mass murder that the song's final lines concerning the impossibility of forgiving and forgetting should be understood.

## Mary O'Malley – *My Role Was That of an Observer (General Robert Ford)*

Mary O'Malley was born in Connemara in 1954 and was educated at University College, Galway. She lectures widely in Europe and America, has written for both radio and television, and is a frequent broadcaster. Her poems have been translated into several languages and she is a member of the Poetry Council for Ireland. She also teaches on the MA in Writing at the National University in Galway.

*My Role Was That of an Observer* appeared in her 2002 collection *The Boning Hall: New and Selected Poems*. It is concerned, as its title suggests, with the type of distancing that can occur when people – most obviously General Robert Ford, Commander of Land Forces in N Ireland in 1972 – wish to avoid the reality of a situation. Mary O'Malley considers this piece one of her own favourites and talks of its relevance to the willed ignorance of many in the South concerning the conflict in the North: 'There is often a particular kind of distancing that goes on in many parts of the South, as if those events were from another country.'

### Kathleen Patton – *Derry's Thirteen*
Kathleen Patton (née Crawford) was born in Porthall, near Lifford in County Donegal. She wrote *Derry's Thirteen* on the evening of 30 January 1972 and according to her family, she added the name of each victim as they were announced on preliminary news reports; hence the inconsistencies in several of the victims' names and ages. The poem was recorded as a monologue around Easter of the same year. Donated to the collection by the Patton family, this poem is the earliest known poetic response to Bloody Sunday.

### Aaron Phelan – *Futility Reigns*
Originally from Belfast, Aaron Phelan says he often feels compelled to write as a means of highlighting the injustice of life in the North. He said writing gives him the means to 'stand up and shout on their behalf.' A retired civil servant, Aaron always kept up to date with the progress of the Saville Inquiry and took an active interest in the subject through books and the recent films. He wrote *Futility Reigns* in Derry around the time of the 2005 anniversary. Its almost overwhelmed bleakness and its imagery owe something to WH Auden's famous elegy *Funeral Blues*.

## Tony Ramsay – *Monday, 31 January 1972*

Tony Ramsay was born in Cromore Gardens in Creggan and was nine years old at the time of Bloody Sunday. Ramsay wrote *Monday, 31 January 1972* around the thirtieth anniversary, when strong emotions were stirred as he watched one of the two Bloody Sunday films on release that year.

The poem is fascinating as it explores the days after the event rather than the event itself. The centrepiece of the poem is a naming of the dead framed on the one hand by the closedown of Derry on the Monday, and on the other by the placing of the coffins in St Mary's Chapel on the Tuesday and the funerals on the Wednesday. The manner in which the dead are named is interesting for the way in which this part litany, part antiphon marks a transition from the world of media reporting into that of prayer; from a public identifying of the dead into a more intimate communal mourning of neighbours, relatives, and colleagues.

## Amanda C Rowe – *William Nash*

Amanda Christine Rowe, originally from Creggan Heights in Derry, was born in 1981. Her paternal grandmother's cousin, Bernard McGuigan, was killed on Bloody Sunday and she attended her first Bloody Sunday commemorative march at the age of twelve. Fuelled by an interest in the subject, Amanda delved into Irish history in general and Bloody Sunday in particular.

Amanda felt compelled to write *William Nash* while doing her homework one night in 1995 and subsequently showed it to John Kelly, brother of Michael Kelly, who subsequently invited her to take part in the campaign process for the new public inquiry. She is now a qualified nursery nurse.

Focusing on a single victim, the piece emphasises the fact that Bloody Sunday took away the lives of distinct individuals:

individuals who had their own concerns, quite distinct from the politics of Civil Rights or anti-Internment. It is in this perhaps obvious but nonetheless crucial awareness that the poignancy of the poem resides.

### Tommy Sands – *Sunday, Bloody Sunday*
Tommy Sands from Rostrevor in County Down is one of Ireland's foremost songwriters and performers. Pete Seeger has described him as 'the most powerful songwriter in Ireland.' Sands is also a social-activist and has just completed a CD written with Protestant and Catholic schoolchildren about their own experiences of growing up in Northern Ireland. During the Good Friday Agreement talks, his impromptu performance with a group of children and Lambeg drummers was described by former Northern Ireland Deputy First Minister Seamus Mallon as 'a defining moment in the Peace Process.'

*Sunday, Bloody Sunday* is a quiet and thoughtful meditation on the events of the day, and on how those events shattered the marchers' optimism for peaceful change in the North. It was written in 1992.

### Scott MX Turner – *1 Para*
Scott MX Turner is a Brooklyn-based writer who plays guitar with the punk band The Devil's Advocates. He has written for *Left Turn*, *Forward Motion*, *Freedom Road*, *Lurch*, *Newsday*, and *The City Sun*.

*1 Para* appeared on the SNIPERS IN DERELICT HOUSES CD, a fund-raising project for the Pat Finucane Centre. Perhaps the most striking feature of this hugely energetic piece, in which rap and traditional Irish instruments cohabit quite easily within a rousing punk ethos, is Turner's intricate level of detail concerning both the events and the contexts of 30 January 1972.

### James Wray – *Untitled*

This poem was donated to the collection by the family of Jim Wray, who died in Glenfada Park after having been shot twice in the back. Although they can't be certain, the Wray family have always presumed that their father James wrote the piece. A handwritten version of the poem was found among his possessions after his death. Evidence for the poem being written in the days following the murder of his son can be gleaned from the line in the first stanza that states *There in the Bogside on Sunday.*

If the poem was in fact the work of James Wray, then it is an invaluable addition to this collection as the only work from a bereaved parent and, indeed, the only piece written from the perspective of a First Battalion Paratrooper. This final point itself is a remarkable facet of a poem that achieves an astounding act of empathy. It stands as a measured articulation of the soldier's awareness of the enormity of his crime.

### Martin Wray – *That Fateful Day*

Martin Wray wrote *That Fateful Day* in tribute to his uncle, Jim Wray, who died on Bloody Sunday. Although written over three decades later, this unashamedly simple poem returns with a forceful intensity to the impressions left by the events of the day. Wray's poem articulates the working of traumatised memory in which, as critic Cathy Caruth says, 'An overwhelming violent event or events that are not fully grasped as they occur . . . return later in repeated flashbacks, nightmares, and other repetitive phenomena.' In its continued questioning of the reason for the men's deaths *that fateful day*, the poem appears caught in that anxious limbo induced by the British state's refusal to recognise its responsibility.